NEW YORK REVIEW BOOKS
C L A S S I C S

LOST TIME

JÓZEF CZAPSKI (1896–1993), a painter and writer, and an eyewitness to the turbulent history of the twentieth century, was born into an aristocratic family in Prague and grew up in Poland under czarist domination. After receiving his baccalaureate in Saint Petersburg, he went on to study law at Imperial University and was present during the February Revolution of 1917. Briefly a cavalry officer in World War I, decorated for bravery in the Polish-Soviet War, Czapski went on to attend the Academy of Fine Arts in Kraków and then moved to Paris to paint. He spent seven years in Paris, moving in social circles that included friends of Proust and Bonnard, and it was only in 1931 that he returned to Warsaw, and began exhibiting his work and writing art criticism. When Germany invaded Poland in September 1939, Czapski sought active duty as a reserve officer. Captured by the Germans, he was handed over to the Soviets as a prisoner of war, though for reasons that remain mysterious he was not among the twenty-two thousand Polish officers who were summarily executed by the Soviet secret police. Czapski described his experiences in the Soviet Union in two books: *Memories of Starobielsk* (forthcoming from NYRB) and *Inhuman Land* (available from NYRB), the latter of which describes his continuing efforts to find out what had happened to his missing and murdered colleagues. Unwilling to live in postwar communist Poland, Czapski set up a studio outside of Paris. His essays appeared in *Kultura*, the leading intellectual journal of the Polish emigration that he helped establish; his painting underwent a great final flowering in the 1980s. Czapski died, nearly blind, at ninety-six.

ERIC KARPELES is a painter who writes about visual and literary aesthetics. He is the author of *Paintings in Proust: A Visual Companion to* In Search of Lost Time and *Almost Nothing: The 20th-Century Art and Life of Józef Czapski* and is a fellow of the Czesław Miłosz Institute at Claremont McKenna College.

LOST TIME

Lectures on Proust in a Soviet Prison Camp

JÓZEF CZAPSKI

Translated from the French by
ERIC KARPELES

NEW YORK REVIEW BOOKS

New York

THIS IS A NEW YORK REVIEW BOOK
PUBLISHED BY THE NEW YORK REVIEW OF BOOKS
435 Hudson Street, New York, NY 10014
www.nyrb.com

First published in the French language as *Proust contre la déchéance: Conférences au camp de Griazowietz* by Les Éditions Noir sur Blanc

Library of Congress Cataloging-in-Publication Data
Names: Czapski, Jozef, 1896–1993, author. | Karpeles, Eric, writer of introduction, translator.
Title: Lost time : lectures on Proust in a Soviet prison camp / by Jozef Czapski ; introduction and translated by Eric Karpeles.
Description: New York : New York Review Books Classics, [2018].
Identifiers: LCCN 2018024070 (print) | LCCN 2018028507 (ebook) | ISBN 9781681372594 (epub) | ISBN 9781681372587 (paperback)
Subjects: LCSH: Proust, Marcel, 1871–1922. À la recherche du temps perdu | Proust, Marcel, 1871–1922—Aesthetics. | Prisoners' writings, Polish—Translations into English. | BISAC: LITERARY CRITICISM / European / French.
Classification: LCC PQ2631.R63 (ebook) | LCC PQ2631.R63 A7848 2018 (print) | DDC 843/.912—dc23
LC record available at https://lccn.loc.gov/2018024070

ISBN 978-1-68137-258-7
Available as an electronic book; ISBN 978-1-68137-259-4

Printed in the United States of America on acid-free paper.
10 9 8 7 6 5 4

for Steven Barclay
and
Mikołaj Nowak-Rogoziński

CONTENTS

TRANSLATOR'S INTRODUCTION

There is some Proust in me, and through Proust,
bit by bit, I become aware of my own possibilities.
— *Józef Czapski, wartime journal entry*

MOST READERS will have picked up this book in response
to the name Marcel Proust. Such was the case for me when
I first came upon the original French version. Studies of
Proust's life and work continue to proliferate: twentieth- and
twenty-first-century literature is unthinkable without Proust;
his eminence is indisputable. By contrast, the Polish painter
and writer Józef Czapski (1896–1993) is virtually unknown
to readers of English, yet when I first read this slender volume
he lingered in my mind, a presence of sufficient interest to
eclipse, albeit momentarily, the blinding sun of Proust. This
book's resonant power derives in part from what it tells us
about the Parisian novelist, but it is the particulars of Czapski's celebration of him that fascinate.

A titled aristocrat by birth, Czapski first arrived in Paris
from Kraków in 1924, a penniless painter at the start of a
long career. (His family's estates and large fortune had been
seized by the newly amalgamated Soviet Union.) A great
reader, he immersed himself in contemporary French writing. Proust, already legendary, had been dead for little more
than a year. Randomly picking up one of the early volumes

of *À la recherche du temps perdu*, Czapski was initially put off by what he found to be an excess of style, but trying again not many months later, in the aftermath of a failed romance, Czapski would find in Proust's novel the intense release that he required. Burying himself in its pages, he developed a profound admiration for the work that would never diminish.

Over the years, his growing circle of Parisian acquaintances came to include several of Proust's old friends. The poet Léon-Paul Fargue entertained Czapski with stories of the elusive writer who lived as a recluse (a recluse who liked, occasionally, to dine at the Ritz). François Mauriac, novelist and critic, welcomed the young Polish painter into a group taking up the cause of spirituality in modern art. Daniel Halévy, twenty-four years Czapski's senior, had been the recipient of several audacious love letters from Proust while they were still schoolmates at Lycée Condorcet, as well as the subject of a purple poem called "Pederasty," in which the seventeen-year-old budding writer praised his friend's adolescent beauty and his "sweet limbs." Czapski would remain a loyal friend of Halévy's for over thirty years.

Proust's spirit was perhaps most vividly brought to life through Czapski's affectionate connection with Maria Godebska-Sert, known to one and all as Misia. A great beauty of Polish descent, Misia, the cherished confidante of Coco Chanel and Sergei Diaghilev, reigned supreme in the beau monde for many decades. An accomplished pianist who had known Franz Liszt and studied with Gabriel Fauré, she was a hostess of wit, intelligence, and charm, a source of envy and dismay to every fashionable Parisienne. Misia's zaftig physique and stylish chic are immediately recognizable in dozens of portraits painted by her friends Édouard Vuillard, Pierre Bonnard, Auguste Renoir, Pablo Picasso, and Henri de Toulouse-Lautrec. Her first husband, Thadée Natanson, with his brothers, launched *La Revue blanche*, a sumptuously illustrated literary journal in whose pages their precocious friend Marcel Proust published his first writings. In *À la recherche*, Misia would be transformed into the exotic Princess Yourbeletieff.

With a characteristic mixture of reluctance and determination, Czapski approached this paragon of high society to ask if she would consider hosting an event to benefit his small band of struggling Polish painters, each of whom dreamed of prolonging their stay in Paris. Heartily agreeing, Misia persuaded Picasso to help; together they drew up a list of distinguished guests to invite. *Le tout Paris* turned out for the occasion and the evening was a success. Artists' models circulated among the crowd draped only in flowers; a raucous jazz band played until dawn. A swarm of grandees materialized, including the Comte and Comtesse de Gramont, the Duc and Duchesse d'Alba, and the Marquis de Polignac. The final volume of *À la recherche* had not yet been published, but Czapski found himself rubbing shoulders with the exalted denizens of Proust's fabled Faubourg Saint-Germain.

Thirteen years later, the "low, dishonest decade" of the thirties came to an end. Czapski was back in Poland, a forty-three-year-old reserve officer defending his country from two invading armies. He was captured in a battle fighting the Germans, yet he and his regiment found themselves taken prisoner by the Red Army. This was unexpected; war had never been declared between the Soviet Union and Poland. Only weeks earlier, a secret alliance had been signed in Moscow by Hitler and Stalin's ministers of foreign affairs,

Joachim von Ribbentrop and Vyacheslav Molotov. The two great powers conspired in the destruction of Polish sovereignty. On September 1, 1939, German armies crossed Poland's western and northern fronts on land and in the air, followed on September 17 by nearly a million Soviet soldiers violating nine hundred miles of Poland's eastern frontier. According to the terms of the covert treaty, the Nazis rounded up rank and file military prisoners for slave labor while the Bolsheviks laid claim to the Polish Army's officer class, soon to be slated for execution.

Soviet authorities were determined to eliminate any threat to their dominion. In the weeks between April 5 and May 5, 1940, roughly twenty-two thousand Polish officers and cadets were murdered at several sites, on orders signed by Stalin and Lavrenty Beria, his chief of secret police. One prisoner of war after another was handcuffed and taken away to be shot with a single bullet in the back of the head. In remote locations, mass burial pits were dug by bulldozers every night for four weeks, piled with bloodied corpses stacked twelve high, then backfilled with dirt and planted over with pine saplings.

Inexplicably, Czapski's life, and those of 395 of his fellow prisoners, had been spared. The surviving officers represented nearly all that remained of Polish military leadership. From various detention centers, these select men were transferred to one camp, a prison established on the derelict grounds of a dynamited Orthodox convent in Gryazovets, once a site of holy pilgrimage, 250 miles northeast of Moscow. The state security police, the NKVD, were their jailers; political operatives had supplanted army command.

Among the prisoners at Gryazovets nothing was known of the executions of their compatriots. Freezing, exhausted from overwork, on the brink of starvation, the men hardly thought of themselves as survivors. Referred to by the camp administration as "former officers of the former Polish army," they struggled to keep their spirits alive and their morale strong, actively resisting the ceaseless attempt to break them down and convert them to the Bolshevik cause. For relief from the relentless misery, the men devised an ongoing series of talks to be given in the evenings before bunking down, each speaker choosing a subject dear to his heart. History, geography, architecture, sports, and ethnography were among the offerings by specialists and amateurs in their respective fields. Czapski volunteered to speak about the development of modern French painting from David to Courbet. In preparation for those talks, he formed the idea of devoting a series of lectures to Proust and *À la recherche du temps perdu*. The officers had no books or other source material with which to research their subjects. Czapski would later write, "Each of us spoke about what he remembered best," and found that a prisoner's constant state of vigilance was surprisingly conducive to the reclamation of memories.

What Czapski remembered best was the quintessential book of remembering. Opening his mind to the narrative's flow, whole scenes from Proust's novel eventually resurfaced, in many instances nearly verbatim. Pulling passages out of thin air, Czapski reenacted the very endeavor of *À la recherche*. "After a certain length of time," he wrote, "facts and details emerge on the surface of our consciousness which we had not the slightest idea were filed away somewhere in our brains."

These memories rising from the subconscious are fuller, more intimately, more personally tied one to the other.

I came to understand why the importance and the creativity of Proust's involuntary memory is so often emphasized. I observed how distance—distance from books, newspapers, and millions of intellectual impressions of normal life—stimulates that memory. Far away from anything that could recall Proust's world, my memories of him, at the beginning so tenuous, started growing stronger and then suddenly with even more power and clarity, completely independent of my will.

Czapski's retrieval of Proust's world "completely independent of my will" echoes the effort the adult narrator makes in *À la recherche* to identify the mysterious associations rising in him after having tasted a morsel of madeleine dunked in a cup of tisane. At first, all he can muster is a flimsy store of memories of childhood holidays at his Aunt Léonie's, "as though all Combray had consisted of but two floors joined by a slender staircase, and as though there had been no time there but seven o'clock at night." He's trapped between actively encouraging the formation of a memory triggered by the taste of tea and cake, and passively accepting that it must materialize of its own accord, acknowledging that "the truth I am seeking lies not in the cup but in myself." His senses ultimately triumph over his power of reasoning and the narrator is granted access to treasures buried deep in himself, yielding "all the flowers in our garden and in M. Swann's park, and the water-lilies on the Vivonne and the good folk of the village and their little dwellings and the parish church and the whole of Combray and of its surroundings."

Proustian methodology cannot be codified; Czapski learned to let the book come back to him without forcing it. Undertaking this process of reclamation, he came to understand that the true search of *À la recherche* is not for what one can remember, but for what one has forgotten. Samuel Beckett insisted that "the man with a good memory does not remember anything because he does not forget anything," and claimed therefore that Proust "had a bad memory." A good memory is "uniform, . . . an instrument of reference instead of discovery." Like Proust's journey, Czapski's was one of discovery, and affirmation.

> I recall with gratitude that around forty of my companions gathered for my French lectures. They came into that chamber at twilight, dressed in *fufaika** and wet shoes. I can still see them packed together underneath portraits of Marx, Lenin, and Stalin, worn out after having worked outdoors in temperatures dropping as low as minus forty-five degrees, listening intently to lectures on themes very far removed from the situation where we currently found ourselves.

Lost Time is a transcription of the talks he gave about Proust to his fellow officers. Having read *À la recherche* in French, he strove to recall it in French, and so gave his talks in French. Two friends from among the assembled listeners agreed to transcribe his talks some time after the lectures had been given to the larger group. Czapski dictated an abridged version to these two scribes. "In our canteen, in the great monastery's refectory stinking of dirty dishes and cabbage, I dictated part of these lectures under the watchful eye of a *politruk*† who suspected us of writing something

*Quilted cotton jackets worn by Soviet prisoners.
†A roving Soviet informer.

politically treasonous." Technically speaking, the book in your hand was not written by Józef Czapski. He never sat down to commit to paper the words that appear in this volume, but two separate handwritten dictations would eventually be converted into two sets of typewritten pages.

Czapski's talks, and our knowledge of the circumstances under which they were given, have been handed down to us in this form. Further details remain difficult to verify. We know that Soviet censors monitored all public gatherings in every prison camp, disallowing the presentation of any potentially seditious (i.e., anti-communist) material. Any spoken text had to be submitted in written form for prior approval. It seems highly unlikely that this text would have been handed to a censor for scrutiny because it could not be expected that a Soviet functionary would be able to read French. And we know from Czapski that this text was transcribed *after* the fact of his having given the lectures, not before. How was this procedural detail overcome? Over how many days or weeks did he give his lectures? How many did he give in all? "I dictated *part of these lectures*," he wrote (my italics). How much more material was there in his original presentations? When were the handwritten transcriptions typed up, where, and by whom? A typewriter would not have been available to prisoners in the camp. How did these pages, in any form, manage to leave the USSR, and in whose possession? Questions pile up, one uncertainty proposing another.

Under the spell of Czapski's compelling voice, however, they subside. We must be grateful for what we do have and accept that we cannot know all. As Proust asserted in *Contre Sainte-Beuve*, "what the intellect offers us under the name of the past is not the past. The past is hidden outside the realm of our intelligence and beyond its reach." After the war, Czapski would supervise a Polish translation of these lectures, publishing them under the title *Proust w Griazowcu* (*Proust at Gryazovets*). The text of his talks would not be published in the original French until 1987, almost half a century after they were given. My translation has been made from this first French edition (*Proust contre la déchéance*), in consultation with the surviving sets of typewritten pages found in Czapski's archive at The Princes Czartoryski Library in Kraków.

———

He chose a casual, conversational tone for his talks. Wearing his learning lightly, he didn't burden his listeners with an excess of esoteric knowledge. Nevertheless he was speaking to a cadre of exceedingly well-educated men; he could slip in a quotation from *Athalie*, Racine's final tragedy, with full expectation that it would be familiar to his audience. His touch was subtle and sure, tempered with humility. He expertly choreographed the thrust and parry of two distinct narratives in his talks—the novelist's and his own. Recounting his first reading of Proust's novel in the spring of 1926, when he had been suffering from typhoid fever and heartbreak, he claimed:

> I was almost drowning in Proust. I had gone to stay with my uncle who at the time was a professor at the University of London. I lived at his place, a small townhouse with a small garden. I would spend all day stretched out on a chaise longue, baking in the sun. There I opened Proust, beginning with *Albertine disparue*, and plunged into his work. I read him all the time.

The bleak surroundings at Gryazovets differed radically from the sun-dappled backdrop of his early enthusiasm. Czapski's determination to engage his fellow prisoners in so unlikely a pairing of content and context reveals a good deal about his own buoyant character and spirit. Who, from the outside, would ever conceive of Proust's stories of the supremely privileged as a subject suitable for an audience of famished, lice-ridden, frostbitten prisoners of war huddled together in bombed-out buildings?

The lectures Czapski gave were unscripted. In preparation, he mapped out a cosmology of Proust, summoning his considerable skills as a visual artist to create schematic drawings in a series of prison notebooks. Intended to be used as aide-mémoire, the sheets he covered with information did not represent any kind of text to be spoken; each page was a carefully constructed nesting ground from which ideas might take flight. The pages are a hybrid of writing and drawing, of thinking and composing. Part blueprint, part stimulant, they represent the frenzied order—or the ordered frenzy?— of his cluttered, cultured mind. Nearly indecipherable at first glance, they gradually reveal their purpose and help us better understand Czapski's plan of attack. Calling on deep reserves of historical knowledge, he put his critical thinking skills into play and hand-lettered several wide-ranging conceptual diagrams. And though his talks were to be given in French, his diagrams were primarily written in Polish. In pencil, colored pencil, watercolor, and ink, the diagrams are packed with references to artistic movements, historical personages, and fictional characters; with the names of writers, painters, philosophers, and musicians; with Proustian icons and biblical allusions. As if throwing a cocktail party for notable ideas, he invited critics, artists, designers, and aristocrats to mix with literary terms (realism, naturalism, romanticism), abstract categories (love, life, compositional methods), and decorative arts (stained glass, still life, Gothic sculpture). The Ballets Russes and cubism appear, as well as Goethe's autobiography, *Dichtung und Wahrheit* (*Poetry and Truth*). A tiny sketch of a haystack is meant to prompt his recall of the phrase "*si le grain ne meurt*," a reference to John 12:24, and the title of André Gide's biography: "Except a grain of wheat fall into the ground and die, it abideth alone; but if it die, it bringeth forth much fruit." These lines, which appear in the very last pages of the very long novel, would figure in Czapski's discussion of the foundations of creativity. His far-flung thoughts on Proust, abidance, and death stretched across time from the Gospels to Gide.

Next to the words "grandeur and misery" written in Polish, the word "resurrection" is inscribed in Cyrillic script in the upper right corner of one diagram. (Having passed his baccalaureate in St. Petersburg, Czapski was fluent in Russian as well as French, Polish, and German.) "Resurrection" is a word that recurs throughout his talks. He cites Tolstoy's late novel *Resurrection* as an example of a work whose moralizing concerns Proust considered antithetical to art. The act of resurrection figures prominently in his retelling of the story of the death of Proust's character Bergotte, a writer whose life and work flash before his eyes as he is dying. But perhaps most significantly, in summing up his talks on *À la recherche*, Czapski presents resurrection as the engine that drives Proust's poetics of memory, fueled by the philosopher Henri Bergson's ideas on intuition. Certainly, involuntary memory is in itself a kind of resurrection, bringing the past back to life, "taking on form and solidity." The narrator of *À la recherche*, exposed to "the existence of a realm of awareness beyond the ordinary" in the novel's final volume, is finally able to recognize his vocation as a writer. He sees that, in his role as an artist, he has the power to save the fragile, foolish, mortal beings surrounding him in the ballroom of the new Princesse de Guermantes. They will all return to life in the book he now intends to write, resurrected from his own wasted years by his newfound powers of observation. In a similar way, Czapski's eventual decision to publish his lectures served to rescue his fellow prisoners from oblivion and, by extension, revive the memory of their murdered comrades. Czapski would continue reading Proust for decades; every reading brought his lost friends back to life.

Czapski's talks introduced a breath of humanity into an inhuman environment. The intent of the Soviets was to destroy any vestige of Polish identity these men clung to, to expunge any trace of freethinking in them, whether political, intellectual, or personal. The strategy was to supplant one belief system with another by means of force—to shatter the prisoners' ideals, then reconstruct them with the glue of communist ideology. This process failed. Despite an arsenal of brutal methods, psychological intimidation, and physical threats used against them, the cadre of Polish officers at Gryazovets refused to succumb. Initially taking up *À la recherche du temps perdu* on the basis of aesthetic inquiry, Czapski soon recognized its value as a practical template for survival. The lectures offered a viable counterpoint to the repeated interrogations the men were forced to endure. His lectures were an act of resistance, stimulating the recovery and retention of personal memories that could protect and defend his colleagues from the attempt to deprive each of them of a sense of self.

The very words *temps perdu*, lost time, must have resonated with heightened significance. Czapski's lectures on *À la recherche du temps perdu* may have reinforced the poignancy of his audience's sense of loss, but the subtext was a rallying cry for making the most of the time at hand. Presenting Proust as a bulwark against fear and desperation, he shepherded his companions towards the French novelist's promise of recovery, of *le temps retrouvé*, towards the hope of finding time again.

———

Throughout war-torn Europe, civilian and military prisoners in other Soviet and German camps experienced similar revelations in the act of reading. Jorge Semprún, a Spanish writer working with anti-Franco forces in France, was arrested by the Gestapo and shipped to Buchenwald, where, he declared, he was saved by his focus on Goethe and Giraudoux. Yevgenia Ginzburg, a teacher and Communist Party member accused of Trotskyist sympathies, drew strength from Pushkin as she fought to stay alive in the Siberian Gulag. In his book *If This Is a Man*, Italian chemist and writer Primo Levi described the unexpected emergence of a jumble of lines of *terza rima* from *The Divine Comedy* as he was shouldering a vessel filled with a hundred pounds of murky soup out to a work detail in the fields at Auschwitz, a teenaged prisoner from Strasbourg at his side. "The canto of Ulysses. Who knows how or why it comes into my mind?" Levi struggled to identify the exact Italian words of the twenty-sixth canto of the *Inferno* so he could put them into French for his Alsatian companion, who had never before heard of Dante:

"Open sea," "open sea" (*mare aperto*), I know it rhymes with "deserted" (*diserto*): "... and with that small company of those who never had deserted me," but I no longer remember if it comes before or after.... As if I, too, were hearing it for the first time: like the blast of a trumpet, like the voice of God. For a moment I forget who I am and where I am.

The act of remembering leads Levi to the great reward of forgetting. Everything falls away, he no longer knows who or where he is. Amid the unspeakable horrors of Auschwitz, oblivion, however fleeting, was a gift of incalculable price. When one is ordered to stand naked during routine body searches, remembered lines of poetry, details of paintings, or phrases of music cannot be confiscated by guards in search of more material treasure.

In other Soviet prisons, two readers of Proust had one great advantage over Czapski: actual volumes of *À la recherche* fell into their hands. At a forced labor camp in Kolyma, a remote Siberian Gulag, Russian writer Varlam Shalamov hoarded details about what he was enduring with the avidity of a starving man devouring food. A great master of the short story, Shalamov is like Chekhov in hell. A fifteen-hundred-page collection of his stories includes many with deceptively unassuming titles: "A Letter," "Cherry Brandy," "The Wheelbarrow." His muted voice resonates with the poverty of his expectations. The constraints on his imagination continually reshape his understanding of the depths of brutality and tenderness. One story, simply called "Marcel Proust," tells of his having stumbled, inconceivably, onto a copy of *Le Côté de Guermantes* at the bottom of a package of clothing sent to a doctor at his camp. Shalamov seized the volume and began to work his way through it, ravenously. Days of reading went by. Distracted by a question put to him by a fellow prisoner, he put the book down on a bench where he had been sitting and reading. Turning back to resume, he found it was gone. Theft was a reality of prison life, but Shalamov had managed to hold onto the book as long as he could. During that time he had sought out quiet corners to read, avoiding his barracks for many days. "Proust," he wrote, "was more valuable than sleep."

The Polish poet and literary critic Aleksander Wat was held deep inside Moscow's notorious Lubyanka prison. Surprisingly, complete private libraries seized from the homes of counterrevolutionary enemies of the state were made available to prisoners. Coming across a Russian volume of *Du côté de chez Swann*, the first book that had been his to read in over a year, Wat digested it hungrily. The edition he found included an introduction by the Marxist literary critic Anatoly Lunacharsky, who praised Proust's genius on the basis of the novel's "scathing descriptions of decadent capitalism." For Wat, the impact of reading Proust was stunning: it helped him to realize that "my entire value system had not been destroyed."

> Reading had a twofold effect in Lubyanka...books stimulated a keen desire for life, life of any sort, at any cost...an insatiable desire to live in freedom, even if that were the miserable freedom of the camps....A second and opposite effect of reading was that it disordered a prisoner's mental structure by causing him to experience two entirely different realities simultaneously: the world of books—free, full of movement, light, change, colorful, Heraclitean—and the world where time stood still, lost all sensation in captivity, and faded into a dirty gray. The sum total of both opposed effects

worked to the investigator's advantage because it disturbed the victim's entire soul.

In his memoir, *My Century*, Wat recalled reading books in prison as

> one of the greatest experiences of my life. Not because they allowed me an escape but because, to a certain extent, they transformed me, influenced and shaped me greatly. It was the way I read those books; I came at them from a completely new angle. And from then on I had a completely new understanding, not only of literature, but of everything.

Czapski experienced a comparably intense reaction while reading whatever books circulated in the camps. In an essay entitled "USSR: 1939–1942," he wrote:

> I don't think I ever read with such attention. The awakening of Stiva Oblonsky in his study after his wife discovers his infidelity [in *Anna Karenina*], the faces of peasants in the scene of the strike in Balzac's *The Peasants* as if painted by Ribera, and above all the scene in *Tess of the d'Urbervilles* where Tess, in the depths of despair, wakes up on the edge of the forest and sees traces of blood nearby and further on bloodied, wounded pheasants. I admit with shame, it was as if those experiences of literature for which I was so hungry were often more powerful than the fall of Paris or the bombing of London, which the Soviet radio reported with evident satisfaction.

The translator's job is to address Czapski's words on the page. Understandably, the words he remembered were not always exactly those Proust composed. I have clung closely to the record of what Czapski spoke at Gryazovets, true to his memory of Proust, if not entirely true to Proust. A few minor inaccuracies dot the text: Czapski locates a crucial party scene at the novel's end in the wrong mansion of the Guermantes family. He evokes a painting by Botticelli in place of the one by Mantegna described by Swann. He hazards a guess about where in the novel the first meeting took place between the narrator and Bergotte, but proposes the wrong volume. Recalling a scene between Swann and a lover of his from before the time he took up with Odette, Czapski refers to the woman as Jeanne. He has not misremembered her name, he has simply provided her with one, which Proust had failed to do. These errors and gaps gain luster for what they reveal about the unfathomable workings of memory.

At the very center of one of the diagrams Czapski drew in preparation for his talks, we find the title *Du côté de chez Swann* circled in a halo of green pencil. Underneath, a constellation of references to key events and characters from Proust's first volume takes shape, all noted in Polish: "mother's kiss," "grandmother (after the rain)," "aunts—wine," "stained glass windows of the Guermantes." All of these orbit about that latent center of Proustian recall, the madeleine, the preeminent symbol of Proust in our popular culture. But whenever Czapski referred to this scallop-shaped butter cake, the pride of pastry in Illiers-Combray, he notated it as "brioche" instead. At this preliminary stage of planning for his talks, the word madeleine seemed to have eluded him entirely.

It is also ironic that Czapski, a painter, mistakes a crucial color in his retelling of Proust's story of Bergotte, the writer who rises from his sickbed in order to attend an exhibition of paintings by Dutch masters. Standing before Vermeer's *View of Delft*, Bergotte sees "for the first time some small figures in blue, that the sand was pink, and, finally, the precious material of the tiny patch of yellow wall." His eyes lock onto this luminously painted passage, the "little patch of yellow wall," which he feels is "so well painted that it was, if one looked at it by itself, like some priceless specimen of Chinese art." Stunned by what he sees, Bergotte is forced to acknowledge the comparative ineptitude of his own artistic offering. He shudders with regret that he had not made use of such intense color in his writing and repeats the phrase "little patch of yellow wall, little patch of yellow wall" to himself, over and over again. Much of the vocabulary in this episode Proust lifted directly from a text about Vermeer written by his friend, the critic Jean-Louis Vaudoyer. Did Proust knowingly take these phrases and rework them into his text as a tribute to Vaudoyer, or had he simply absorbed them, unwittingly, as his own?

Poring over the typewritten pages of Czapski's talks in the Kraków archive, I counted five references to Bergotte's doleful mantra about the little patch of wall. But in each repetition, Czapski's patch of wall appears as the wrong color. He writes that Bergotte was repeating to himself, "little patch of pink wall, little patch of pink wall." In both sets of typescript, the phrase appears over and over as "*petit pan de mur rose.*" In one of the two sets, the passage remains as transcribed, while in the other, the word *rose* has been lightly crossed out and the word *jaune*, yellow, written above it, though not in Czapski's hand. After the war, when the Polish translation of his text appeared in print, this mistake was corrected. The wall returned to Vermeer's original color—yellow wall, *mur jaune*, *żółty murek* in Polish. The edited version makes the citation once again true to Proust but, poignantly, no longer true to Czapski. The madeleine and the little patch of yellow wall are major foundation stones of the Proustian edifice. Curiously, both slipped Czapski's mind.

These are unusual exceptions. Czapski's memory is otherwise prodigious. He embellishes key scenes with a bounty of vivid details. He describes the narrator's obsession for Gilberte, a young girl with whom he plays after school in the gardens of the Champs-Élysées. One evening, the agitated youngster must wait before being allowed to go out to meet her.

The hero's grandmother, already ill by then, is long delayed coming back from her daily outing in a carriage before dinner. The boy notices his first reaction: "Perhaps Grandmother has had another attack, perhaps she's already dead, and I'll be late for my rendezvous on the Champs-Élysées." To this he adds, with similar distancing objectivity and so-called indifference: "When one loves someone, one loves no one else."

In this passage, Czapski intermingles the conflicted feelings of the novel's hero, his devotion to his beloved grandmother, the conventions of the dinner table, incipient sexual anxiety, infatuation, delusion, and love. The two textual passages inserted in a paraphrased summary of the storyline are nearly word-perfect citations from Proust. Employing this pattern of reference throughout his talks, Czapski encapsulates a scene and weaves into it a direct quotation or two. In this way, the novelist's voice emerges directly in the midst of Czapski's exposition. Proust was widely admired for his ability to recite whole pages of Balzac and Saint-Simon from memory; Czapski displays a similar prowess.

By the time Czapski was taken prisoner, he was already extremely familiar with published commentaries on Proust, having read much of the secondary literature about *À la recherche* that began to appear from the mid-1920s onwards. He made his own contribution early in 1928 with an essay, "Marceli Proust," published in a Polish journal; at the time, he was among a very small number of Poles who had read the entire novel in French. He had also read most of what was available in print of Proust's correspondence with his friends. In his lectures, Czapski refers to assessments of Proust by François Mauriac, Jean Cocteau, André Gide, Ramon Fernandez, Léon-Paul Fargue, and "others which I don't recall." Among those tributes Czapski does not name was one of the first book-length studies to proclaim the arrival of a new literary masterwork: *Marcel Proust: sa vie, son oeuvre* (*Marcel Proust: His Life, His Work*), published in 1925, three years after Proust's death. This text was written by Léon Pierre-Quint, a lawyer, novelist, editor, and publisher who had mixed in the same social world as Proust and become his friend. Both were students of the philosopher Henri Bergson, both had Jewish ancestry. Both were sexually attracted to other men, both were high-functioning medical invalids; Pierre-Quint suffered from the effects of tuberculosis throughout his life.

After Proust's entire novel became available in print in 1927, Pierre-Quint twice expanded his original commentary, in 1928 and again in 1935. From Czapski's 1928 essay we know that he read the first version of Pierre-Quint's study; Czapski cites it as a source.

When I came to the end of Czapski's lectures on Proust for the first time, a flicker of recognition went through me. About the death of Proust, he wrote, "They found him dead in the morning in his bed." The next, and final, sentence of his lectures reads as follows:

On his nightstand a flask of medicine had been overturned, its liquid blackening a little sheet of paper on which had been written that same night, in his fine, nervous handwriting, the name of a not-even-secondary character from *À la recherche*: Forcheville.*

From his extensive reading about Proust, Czapski latched on to this idea of "Forcheville" being among the very last words the great novelist committed to paper before dying. At the end of his account of Proust's life, Pierre-Quint also describes Proust on his deathbed:

Beside him, blackened by one of his numerous medicines whose bottle had overturned, a scrap of paper was found, where, among some illegible words, one could make out the name of Forcheville, one of the secondary characters from his book.†

---

* *"Sur sa table de nuit était renversé un flacon de médicaments dont le liquide avait noirci une tout petite feuille de papier sur laquelle avait été noté cette nuit même de sa fine écriture nerveuse le nom d'un personnage moins que secondaire d'* À la recherche*: Forcheville."*

† *"Auprès de lui, noirci par un des nombreux médicaments dont la bouteille s'était renversée, on trouva un morceau de papier, où, parmi des mots illisibles, on distinguait le nom de Forcheville, un des personnages de second plan de son livre."*

Two words in this sentence—*noirci* (blackened) and *Forcheville*—must have imprinted themselves on me when I read Pierre-Quint's book decades ago, and the odd conjunction of words struck me again the first time I reached the end of Czapski's lectures. I wasn't immediately able to identify the author who had described the deathbed scene so similarly: it took me some time to track down the original source. Thumbing through several linear feet of material concerning the last days of Proust, I finally came across the passage in Pierre-Quint's book and was able to recover something I'd forgotten I knew. I suspect it was Pierre-Quint's still-life-like reconstruction of Proust's bedside table, with its overturned bottle and stained paper, that made a vivid impression on Czapski's painterly cast of mind, as it did on mine. In his lectures, Czapski recycled Pierre-Quint's sentence but neglected referencing its source or, more likely, had forgotten it, in the same way that Proust made use of the "little patch of yellow wall" from the text by Vaudoyer.

References to Forcheville and the darkened piece of paper appear in several later accounts of Proust's sad end. For instance, from the pages of Mauriac's memoir, *Du côté de chez Proust*: "…and we saw, on an envelope stained with tisane, the last illegible words he penned, and only the name Forcheville was decipherable…" At the end of the second volume of George Painter's biography: "…written on the back of an envelope stained by a spilt tisane, in a tragically changed and quavering hand; only a few phrases are legible or intelligible…" Though the scrap of paper is identified as an envelope, and its stain caused by herbal tea rather than by medicine, these accounts also seem traceable back to Pierre-Quint's book. And, like these earlier commentators, Czapski worked on the assumption that the *Forcheville* Proust refers to was

Baron de Forcheville, the social-climbing bounder who replaces Swann as Odette's lover, a decidedly secondary character in the novel. All were puzzled by this mysterious reference to such a minor figure at the very end of the novelist's life. George Painter, however, suggests that the Forcheville Proust had in mind in his dying moments was not the vulgar sensualist at all, but the enchanting Mademoiselle Forcheville, the baron's adopted daughter, otherwise known as Gilberte Swann, a character of primary importance. Long after the narrator's juvenile anguish about not being able to meet her in the gardens of the Champs-Élysées faded, Gilberte married Robert de Saint-Loup. Their daughter, Mademoiselle Saint-Loup, is a crowning achievement of Proust's novel, the flesh and blood reconciliation of two previously incompatible "ways." Painter proposes that Gilberte is the Forcheville Proust is thinking of, from a scene near the end of *Albertine disparue* that he had been revising the day before he died. (The reigning biographer-king of Proust, Jean-Yves Tadié, makes no reference to bedside table, overturned medicine bottles, stained papers, or the name Forcheville.)

Though they did not know that more than twenty thousand of their fellow officers had been murdered by the Soviet authorities, the Polish officers at Gryazovets were keenly aware that their captors might kill them. With a confidence in the perpetuity of great art, Czapski addressed this atmosphere of hovering mortality by ending his series of lectures with a description of the death of Bergotte, followed by an account of Proust's own demise. He described the novelist working against the clock to complete his book, "sealed in his cork-lined room, as if in a coffin, curtains drawn, at death's door, still trying to enrich and deepen his work, line by line.... Death came and took him as he deserved to be taken, while still hard at work."

Only after many barren years had passed was Proust's hero, convinced of his lack of talent, finally able to discover his vocation as a writer. Czapski elaborates:

> All this he sees with new eyes, lucidly, detached, and from a distance; finally he knows what he is meant to do with his life. It's he, and he alone in this crowd, who will make them all come to life again, he knows it with a force of certainty that death has become a matter of indifference to him.

In the presence of a very real threat, the notion of cultivating an indifference to death appealed to Czapski; it formed a critical subtext to what he offered his listeners. He was shrewd enough to realize that, in the larger picture of a world war, the story of what had happened to him and to his compatriots could easily vanish in the wider cataclysm. Facts would be denied actively by the perpetrators and pushed from the minds of survivors who only wanted never to remember. As Czapski prepared his talks, as he gave them, and as he repeated them afterwards for his friends to transcribe, he understood that, for him, any future experience of Proust would be forever linked with Gryazovets. In this way he was able to make the most of *Lost Time*.

———

The transcripts of Czapski's lectures are held in the Princes Czartoryski Library of the National Museum in Kraków.

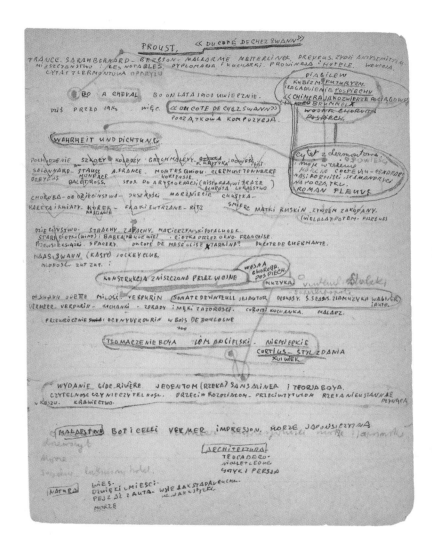

The translation of this diagram appears on the last page of the insert.

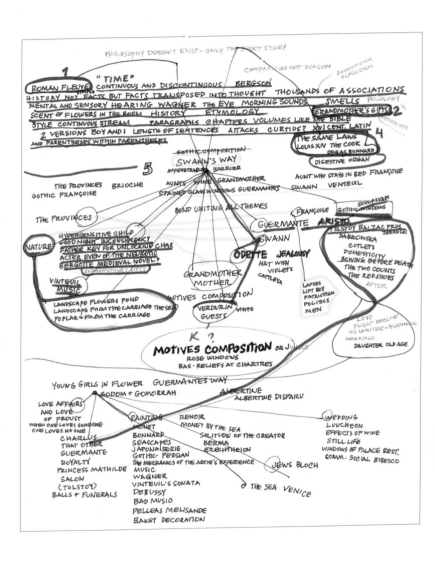

PHILOSOPHY DOESN'T EXIST - ONLY THE SHORT STORY

COMPARISON NOT REASON   ROMANTICISM
                           CLASSICISM

1 "TIME" CONTINUOUS AND DISCONTINUOUS   BERGSON
ROMAN FLEUVE SIMPLE
HISTORY NOT FACTS BUT FACTS TRANSPOSED INTO THOUGHT   THOUSANDS OF ASSOCIATIONS
MENTAL AND SENSORY HEARING WAGNER THE EYE MORNING SOUNDS   SMELLS PHILOLOGY
SCENT OF FLOWERS IN THE ROOM HISTORY   ETYMOLOGY   GRANDMOTHER'S GIFTS **2**
STYLE CONTINUOUS STREAM   PARAGRAPHS CHAPTERS VOLUMES LIKE THE BIBLE   MICROSCOPE
  2 VERSIONS BOY AND I LENGTH OF SENTENCES ATTACKS CURTIUS? XVI CENT. LATIN
AND PARENTHESES WITHIN PARENTHESES   THE SAME LAWS   **4**
                                                  LOUIS XIV THE COOK
                        GOTHIC COMPOSITION   DEGAS BONNARD
                        SWANN'S WAY   DIGESTIVE ORGAN
              5   IMPENETRABLE BARRIER

THE PROVINCES   BRIOCHE   AUNT WHO STAYS IN BED FRANÇOISE
GOTHIC FRANÇOISE   AUNTS WINE GRANDMOTHER
                      STAINED GLASS WINDOWS GUERMANTES   SWANN VENTEUIL

THE PROVINCES   FRANÇOISE GOTHIC SOUVERAINE?
                    BOND UNITING ALL THEMES   WINDOWS
                                         GUERMANTE ARISTO.   TOLSTOY BALZAC PRUS.
NATURE   HYPERSENSITIVE CHILD   SWANN   DABROWSKA ZUKOWSKI
         GOOD NIGHT INCONSISTENCY   CUTLETS
         FATHER KEY FOR UNLOCKING CHAR-   ODETTE JEALOUSY   DOMESTICITY
         ACTER EVEN OF THE NEUROTIC   HAT WITH   BOWING BEFORE DEATH
         BERGOTTE MEDIEVAL NOVEL?   VIOLETS   THE TWO COUNTS
         GRANDMOTHER'S GIFTS   CATTLEYA   THE RED SHOES
VINTEUIL   AFTER
MUSIC   GRANDMOTHER   LAPSES
                    MOTHER   LIFT BOY
LANDSCAPE FLOWERS POND   PATRIOTISM
LANDSCAPE FROM THE CARRIAGE THE SEA MOTIVES COMPOSITION POLITICS   LOVE
POPLARS FROM THE CARRIAGE   VERDURIN   WHITS   MEN   FLIGHT DECLINE
                                   GUESTS   HIS LASSITUDE & TELEPHONING
                                                                     MARRIAGE
                  K ?   DAUGHTER OLD AGE
            MOTIVES COMPOSITION OR JUNGLE
                  ROSE WINDOWS
                  BAS-RELIEFS AT CHARTRES

    YOUNG GIRLS IN FLOWER GUERMANTES WAY
            SODOM + GOMORRAH   ALBERTINE
LOVE AFFAIRS   ALBERTINE DISPARU
AND LOVE
OF PROUST
WHEN ONE LOVES SOMEONE   PAINTING RENOIR   WEDDING
ONE LOVES NO ONE   MONET MONET BY THE SEA   LUNCHEON
  CHARLUS   BONNARD SOLITUDE OF THE CREATOR EFFECTS OF WINE
  THAT OTHER   SEASCAPES BERMA   STILL LIFE
  GUERMANTE   JAPONAISERIE ERECHTHEION   WINDOWS OF PALACE REST.
  ROYALTY   GOTHIC-PERSIAN   COMM. SOCIAL BIBESCO
  PRINCESS MATHILDE   THE MECHANICS OF THE ARTIST'S EXPERIENCE
  SALON   MUSIC   JEWS BLOCH
  (TOLSTOY)   WAGNER
  BALLS + FUNERALS   VINTEUIL'S SONATA
                       DEBUSSY   THE SEA VENICE
                       BAD MUSIC
                       PELLEAS MELISANDE
                       BAKST DECORATION

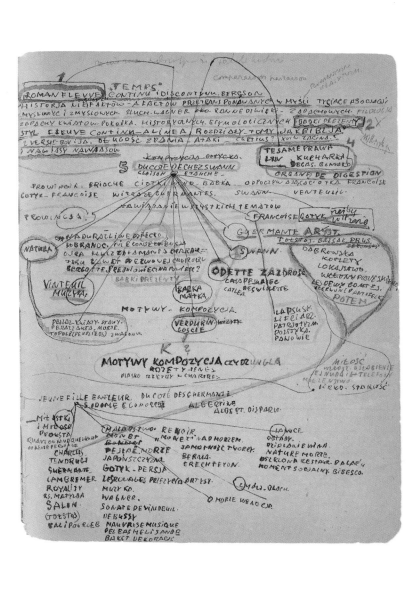

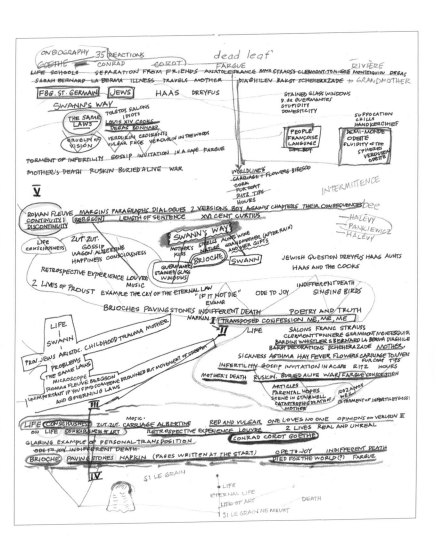

ON BIOGRAPHY 35 REACTIONS · · · · · dead leaf

GOETHE · · · CONRAD · · · COROT · · · FARGUE · · · · RIVIÈRE

LIFE SCHOOLS · · · SEPARATION FROM FRIENDS · · · ANATOLE FRANCE Mme STRAUSS CLERMONT-TONNERE MONTESQUIOU DEGAS
SARAH BERNARD LA BERMA ILLNESS TRAVELS MOTHER · · · DIAGHILEV BAKST SCHEHERAZADE to GRANDMOTHER

FBG. ST. GERMAIN · · · JEWS · · · HAAS · · · DREYFUS

SWANN'S WAY

THE SAME LAWS — TOLSTOY, SALONS · · · STAINED GLASS WINDOWS
IDIOTS · · · P. de GUERMANTES STUPIDITY DOMESTICITY
LOUIS XIV COOKS DEGAS BONNARD
CRUELTY OF VISION · · · VERDURIN CROISSANTS · · · SUFFOCATION CHILLS HANDKERCHIEF
VULGAR FACE VERDURIN IN THE WOODS

PEOPLE FRANÇOISE LANGUAGE LIFT-BOY

DEMI-MONDE ODETTE FLUIDITY OF THE SPHERES VERDURIN ODETTE

TORMENT OF INFERTILITY GOSSIP INVITATION IN A CAPE FARGUE

MOTHER'S DEATH RUSKIN BURIED ALIVE WAR

WORLDLINESS CARRIAGE + FLOWERS BIBESCO CORK FUR COAT RITZ TIPS HOURS

INTERMITTENCE

V

ROMAN FLEUVE MARGINS PARAGRAPHIC DIALOGUES 2 VERSIONS BOY AGAINST CHAPTERS THEIR CONSEQUENCES bee
CONTINUITY / DISCONTINUITY (BERGSON) LENGTH OF SENTENCE XVI CENT CURTIUS

HALÉVY
PANKIEWICZ
HALÉVY

LIFE CONSCIOUSNESS · · · ZUT ZUT. · · · SWANN'S WAY
GOSSIP WAGON ALBERTINE HAPPINESS CONSCIOUSNESS · · · MOTHER'S KISS · · · SMELLS AUNT'S WINE NATURE GRANDMOTHER (AFTER RAIN) AND HER GIFTS

GUERMANTES STAINED GLASS WINDOWS · · · BRIOCHE · · · SWANN

JEWISH QUESTION DREYFUS HAAS AUNTS
HAAS AND THE COOKS

RETROSPECTIVE EXPERIENCE LOUVRE MUSIC

2 LIVES OF PROUST · · · EXAMPLE THE CRY OF THE ETERNAL LAW · · · INDIFFERENT DEATH SINGING BIRDS
"IF IT NOT DIE" EVANG. · · · ODE TO JOY

BRIOCHES PAVING STONES INDIFFERENT DEATH · · · POETRY AND TRUTH

NAPKIN I TRANSPOSED CONFESSION ME, ME, ME
II LIFE

LIFE · · · SALONS FRANZ STRAUSS
SWANN · · · CLERMONT-TONNERE GRAMMONT MONTESQUIOU
PROV. JEWS ARISTOC. CHILDHOOD TRAUMA MOTHER · · · BARDINI WHISTLER & BERNARD LA BERMA DIAGHILE
· · · BAKST DECORATIONS SCHEHERAZADE MOTHER
PROBLEMS · · · SICKNESS ASTHMA HAY FEVER FLOWERS CARRIAGE TOU MEN FUR COAT TIPS
THE SAME LAWS · · · INFERTILITY GOSSIP INVITATION IN A CAPE RITZ HOURS
MICROSCOPE · · · MOTHER'S DEATH RUSKIN. BURIED ALIVE WAR FARGUE CONSCRIPTION
ROMAN FLEUVE BERGSON · · · ARTICLES
UNIMPORTANT IF YOU FIND SOMEONE DROWNED BUT MOVEMENT OF STREAM · · · PARENTAL HOPES
AND GOVERNING LAWS · · · SCENE IN STAIRWELL · · · ROZANOV WEIL
· · · CATASTROPHE DEATH OF · · · TORMENT OF INFERTILITY GOSSIP
· · · MOTHER

III

LIFE CONSCIOUSNESS ZUT ZUT. CARRIAGE ALBERTINE · · · RED AND VULGAR ONE LOVES NO ONE OPINIONS ON VERDURIN II
ON LIFE CONSCIOUSNESS OF ART · · · RETROSPECTIVE EXPERIENCE LOUVRE · · · 2 LIVES REAL AND UNREAL
MUSIC.
GLARING EXAMPLE OF PERSONAL TRANSPOSITION · · · CONRAD COROT GOETHE
ODE TO JOY INDIFFERENT DEATH · · · ODE TO JOY INDIFFERENT DEATH
BRIOCHE PAVING STONES NAPKIN (PAGES WRITTEN AT THE START) · · · DIED FOR THE WORLD (?) FARGUE

IV · · · SI LE GRAIN

• LIFE
ETERNAL LIFE
LIFE OF ART · · · DEATH
SI LE GRAIN NE MEURT

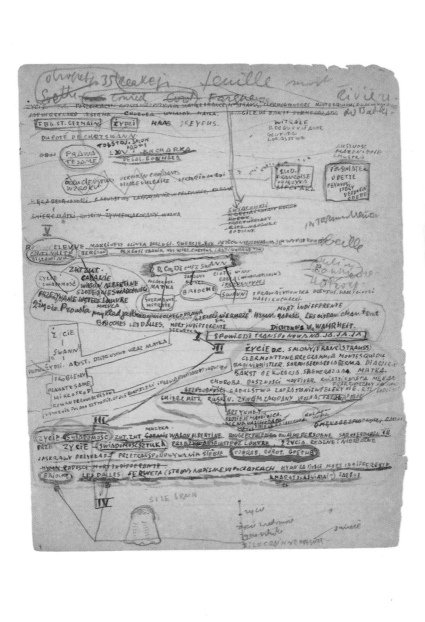

PASCAL   GRANDEUR + MISERY

1 B' (MY CONCLUSIONS)   (NOTHINGNESS of PLEASURE)   NEVER THE TENDENTIOUSNESS
     SCHOPENHAUERISM   PROXIMITY TO CHRISTIANITY   of ŻEROMSKI RESURRECTION
1 of FRANCE ✗ of POETRY,   HAPPINESS   SUFFERING   PEARL
THE WORLD   LOVE   CELEBRATION of the SENSES   HEDONISM
          AMOROUS ADVENTURES   MARRIAGE   (ART)   MONEY
                                         WINE
                                         LUXURY

2 THE WORLD and SWANN   INDIFFERENCE   EGOISM
THE END of SWANN   SHOES   FUNERALS   FATE ODETTE

                                                   CHAINED
        PRIDE   ROCK of
3 NOTHINGNESS PRIDEFUL   GUERMANTES   VERDURIN   AMERICANS   MATTER
                                                 CHARLUS
4 of TIME THE IRREPARABLE OUTRAGE   ODETTE, THE CROWD   GUERMANTES
             PHEDRE   Bois de BOULOGNE   (? ON STILTS
5 FAME   BERMA   SARAH BERNARD
6 LOVE ADVENTURE CHARLUS   PERVERSION MASOCHISM EVERYTHING. ✗   WHEELCHAIR - BLINDNESS
6 ALBERTINE   ODETTE   DON'T EVEN REMEMBER

    CEL.   (ARTIST NOT EVEN   WALL PINK WALL
                                  IDENTIFIED)   DOSTOEVSKY
7 BERGOTTE   DECADENCE   of FORMS of JOY   ILLNESS (VERMEER)
   (GOD) VERMEER   BLESSED SUFFERING   STREET WINGS of ANGELS   DEAD FOR
                                 FARGUE on HIS SUBJECT   STANDING GUARD   GOOD?
   HIS TRIUMPH   HIS DEATH
THEY WILL LIVE.

                          A PEARL   A GRAIN
       8   DEATH of PROUST   ANNOYED
                    MEDICINE CURES   FORCHEVILLE
GRANDEUR + MISERY   INDIFFERENT DEATH

                                           ✗ PRECIOUS WOUND
                                   6   ✗ A BIT MIRED IN
                                           THE FLESH

                                     ✗ SOLITUDE. (BERGOTTE)

✗ ANATOLE FRANCE WROTE FOR PLEASURE
       SUCCESS WITH WOMEN

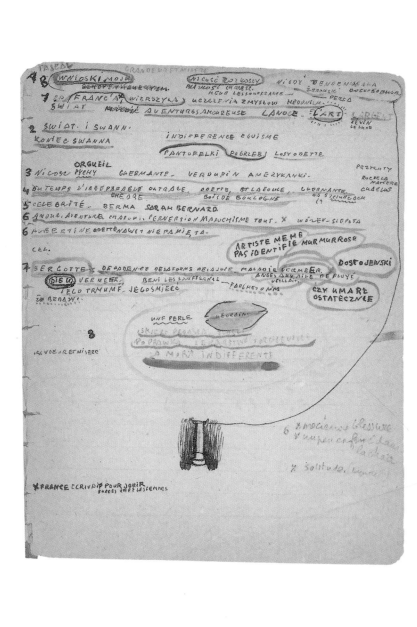

PASCAL   GRANDEUR ET MISÈRE
48 (WNIOSKI MOJE)   (NICOŚĆ ROZKOSZY   NICOŚĆ TENDENCJA CIAŁA
      SCHOPENHAUEROWSKIM   ODRZUCA CHRZEŚĆ.   ZBRODNI BOGOBOJNOŚĆ)
7 2 (FRANCJA, WIERSZYKA) UCZCIĆ VIA ZMYSŁÓW HEDONIZM   PERŁA
   ŚWIAT   MIŁOŚĆ AVENTURES AMOUREUSE LANCE   L'ART   L'ORIENT
                                                        SEVIN
2 ŚWIAT I SWANN   LE LUXE
   KONIEC SWANNA   INDIFFERENCE EGUISME
                      PANTOFELKI POGRZEB LOS ODETTE
      ORGUEIL   PRZYKUTY
3 NICOŚĆ PYCHY GUERMANTE VERDURIN AMERYKANKI   ROCOCO
                                                         MANIÈRE
4 DU TEMPS D'IRRÉPARABLE OUTRAGE ODETTE, ET LAEOULE GUERMANTE CHARLUS
           THÉ ODE   BOIS DE BOULOGNE   VO SZTUKACH
5 CÉLÉBRITÉ - BERMA SARAH BERNARD
6 AMOUR AVENTURE CHARLUS PERVERSION MASOCHISME TOUT . X WÓLEV - ŚLEPOTA
6 PUBERTÉ GNE ODETTE NAWET NIE PAMIĘTA -
   CEL.
                          ARTISTE MÊME
                          PAS IDENTIFIÉ MURMUR ROSE
7 BERCOTTE - DÉCADENCE DÉSIFORME MÉLAISME MALADIE VERMEER   DOSTOJEWSKI
                                            ANGE, AUX AILE DE PLUYE
   (DIEU) VERMEER.   BENI LES SOUFFRANCE VEILLAIT.
   JEGO TRYUMF. JEGO ŚMIERĆ   FORGET ONIM   CZY UMARŁ
   ŻE BĘDĄ Ź   OSTATECZNIE

      3
                      UNE PERLE   HEORDIN
   GRANDEUR ET MISÈRE ŚMIERĆ PRAWDA
                   PO PRAWDĄ LE ARTISTE FORGOT OVERA
                      A MORT INDIFFERENT

                                         6 AMOUR BLESSURE
                                         4 UMPEN ON POUR CHAUD
                                              LA CHAIN
                                         7 SOLITUDE

X FRANCE ÉCRIVAIT POUR JOUIR
         SUCCÈS CHEZ LES FEMMES

PROUST, «DU COTÉ DE CHEZ SWANN»

FRANCE. SARAH BERNARD — BERGSON MALLARMÉ MEITERLINCK DREYFUS. JEWS ANTI SEMITISM
BOURGEOISIE: THE NOTABLES DIPLOMATS AND WOMEN COOKS PROVINCES & HOTELS VENICE
CITATION OF LERMONTOV OF PARIS

DIAGHILEV
CUBISM FUTURISM
THE QUESTION OF SPEED
CHIMERA AS A BEAST OF BURDEN
⑧ BECAUSE ON HORSEBACK BECAUSE HE IMMORTALIZED THE YEAR 1900. SIR LORD BRUMMEL X
«DU COTE DE CHEZ SWANN» WAR DISEASE SPEED
TODAY BEFORE 1914 SO. ORIGINAL COMPOSITION.

TRUTH AND POETRY

ORIGINS SCHOOLS • FRIENDS GABBH HALÉVY ART NOVELS LEFT.
R.CRITIC
SALONNARD. Mme STRAUSS A. FRANCE MONTESQUIOU CLERMONT TONNERRE
MY PAGE HYDRANGEA
DREYFUS BALLETS RUSS. ARISTOCRATIC BEHAVIOR HISTORY STAINED GLASS
STUPIDITY, DOMESTICITY
SICKNESS FROM CHILDHOOD ASTHMA CHILLS HANDKERCHIEF
CARRIAGE FLOWERS CORK-LINED FUR-LINED COAT RITZ DEATH MOTHERS RUSKIN BURIED ALIVE.
WALLS MANY YEARS LATER FARGUES

CITATION OF LERMONTOV
AND MY IMPRESSION • TALES
MORANO COCTEAU — CENDRARS
OUR FORMISTS, SKAMANDARISTS
AT THE START
ROMAN FLEUVE

CHILDHOOD FEARS ODORS MOTHER'S KISS
THE OLD AUNTS (WINE) GRANDMOTHER (AFTER RAIN) AUNT BY WINDOW FRANÇOISE.
FIRST BOOKS WALKS THE MÉSÉGLISE WAY X HAWTHORN DU COTE DE GUERMANTE.
HAAS SWANN (CASTE) JOCKEY CLUB.
CHILDHOOD. ZUT ZUT. :

WAR DISEASE SPEED
CONSTRUCTION DESTROYED BY WAR MUSIC Vinteuil Tables
gad 200ks
CH. SWANN ODETTE LOVE VERDURIN VINTEUIL SONATA AUTHOR DEBUSSY. S. SAENS. BAD MUSIC WAGNER
AND THE GNR
VERMEER VERDURIN MISTRESSES BETRAYALS + TORMENTS OF JEALOUSY WHAT MISTRESSES DO PAINTER

CLEAR REVERSAL OF JUDGMENT VERDURIN IN BOIS de BOULOGNE
TRANS.

BOY'S TRANSLATION ENGLISH TRANS. GERMAN
CURTIUS — SENTENCE STYLE
XVI CENTURY

EDITIONS GIDE RIVIÈRE ONE VOLUME (STREAM) WITHOUT PARAGRAPHS AND BOY'S THEORY
LEGIBILITY OR ILLEGIBILITY AGAINST CHAPTERS AGAINST TITLES A STREAM CONTINUALLY
BASKET FOR SEWING FLOWING

○ PAINTING BOTICELLI VERMER IMPRESSION. SEA JAPONAISERIE
wooden graving Vermer Impression Sea Japanese

sea ARCHITECTURE
TROCADERO-
social VIOLLET LE DUC
luxury hotel GOTHIC + PERSIAN
NATURE COUNTRYSIDE
SOUNDS OF THE CITY
LANDSCAPE FROM CAR VILLAGES LIKE HERDS MOVING
SEA

Over the course of several years, I spent many days in the hushed confines of these imposing rooms carefully comparing the two original typescripts. On my last visit, as I removed each of the two brittle piles from their protective folders and laid them out on the table, I saw that the pages had been filed away upside down. Just before turning them over to bring the typed text face up, I noticed some markings that I had not seen before. On the top page of one of the two upside-down piles I spotted a small, circular mark in purple-bluish ink, the museum's institutional seal. Above the stamp, the document's inventory number was neatly handwritten in ink. The words "Czapski sur Proust" had been inscribed vertically, one word above the other, accompanied by a squiggly flourish. There, on the same sheet, I discovered a charming drawing of an alert, shaggy-haired dog seated in profile, immediately recognizable as the work of Czapski and surely a study of one of the long line of pets he and his sister Marynia kept in their small rooms outside of Paris (see page 88).

Dashed off like thousands of other impromptu sketches over a career of seventy years, this quick ink drawing delighted me. I looked at it for some time. A dog, unlike an adult, or even a well-behaved child, doesn't hold a pose for long. Czapski must have had an impulse to capture this happy, dignified canine while the sweet-looking creature was sitting still, his eyes bright and attentive. Ever prepared, Czapski would have had a pen or pencil near to hand. But paper? Where was his sketchbook? Somewhere else. What could he use? A stack of old paper was in sight, he grabbed a sheet and got the image down quickly, before the dog moved on in search of something to eat, or a toy, or a place to stretch out and sleep. Hardly caring what piece of paper he used, Czapski snagged what was at hand and set to work. The dog's eye is clearly noted in profile, the head noble and erect, a few fuzzy lines for the furry coat—all sketched in less than a minute—and, bingo, a lively rendering of the creature was caught on the page, endearing, loyal, affectionate.

The artist's sharp eyes and swift fingers fulfilled their insatiable need to make sense of the visible world. Lifting a random page from a stack of paper in his bedroom/studio, Czapski made a record of what was there before his eyes. The drawing was made in a moment; soon the dog trotted off, the day wore on. A sheet of yellowed paper that survived a time of ceaseless misery in the charnel house of Soviet Russia, a sheet that on one side held his retelling of Proust's last days, became on the other side, years later, a blank surface for a sketch dashed off in the midst of domestic happiness. The pale hovering shadow of the past merged with the present and then retreated again.

I picked the sheet up and held it in my hands, studying both sides. At some point, Czapski must have done the same thing, before moving on to whatever came next.

—ERIC KARPELES

LOST TIME

TRANSLATOR'S NOTE

Comments in parentheses in the body of the text are Czapski's own. In the rare cases of discrepancy between the two nearly identical typescripts, I have chosen whichever variation I feel best enhances Czapski's narrative.

AUTHOR'S INTRODUCTION

THIS ESSAY on Proust was dictated in the winter of 1940–41 in the cold refectory of an abandoned convent that served as the mess hall of our prison camp at Gryazovets in the Soviet Union.

The subjective quality of these pages and their lack of precision can be explained in part by the fact that I had neither a library nor a single book on my subject; I hadn't seen a book in French since before September 1939. I had only some memories of Proust's work, which I forced myself to recall with relative accuracy. This is not a literary essay in the true sense of the word, but rather the recollection of a work to which I was deeply indebted and which I was not sure of seeing again in my life.

We were four thousand Polish officers crammed into very tight living quarters at Starobielsk, near Kharkov, from October 1939 until the spring of 1940. There we tried to take up a kind of intellectual work that would help us overcome our depression and anguish, and to protect our brains from the rust of inactivity. Several among us began to organize military, historical, and literary lectures. This was judged counterrevolutionary by our overseers at the time, and some of the speakers were deported immediately to unknown destinations. The lectures were not curtailed, however, but carefully continued in secret.

5

In April 1940, the whole camp at Starobielsk was deported to the north in small groups. Two other large camps, at Kozelsk and Ostashkov, were also evacuated at the same time, numbering in all about fifteen thousand people. Of all these prisoners, the only ones ever to be seen again were about four hundred officers and soldiers grouped together at Gryazovets, near Vologda, during the year, 1940–41. We were seventy-nine out of four thousand from Starobielsk. All our other comrades from Starobielsk disappeared without a trace.

Before 1917, Gryazovets had been a place of pilgrimage, a convent. The convent church stood in ruins, destroyed by dynamite. The rooms were filled with skeletal support structures, the bunks, infested with bedbugs, had been occupied previously by Finnish prisoners.

Only here, after numerous appeals, did we receive official permission to continue with our gatherings, on the condition that every speaker present a text to the censor for prior approval. In a small room packed with comrades, each of us spoke about what he remembered best.

The history of books was recounted with rare feeling by a passionate bibliophile from Lwów, Dr. Ehrlich; the history of England, the history of the migrations of peoples, formed the basis of lectures given by Father Kamil Kantak, from Pińsk, former editor of a daily newspaper in Gdańsk and a great admirer of Mallarmé; Professor Siennicki from the Polytechnic School at Warsaw spoke about architectural history; Lieutenant Ostrowski, author of an excellent book on mountain climbing, who had made numerous ascents in the Tatras Mountains, in the Caucasus, and the Cordilleras, spoke to us about South America.

My involvement took the form of a series of talks on

French and Polish painting, as well as on French literature. Convalescing from a serious illness, I was fortunate to find myself excused from hard labor and, except for scrubbing the convent's main staircase and peeling potatoes, I was at liberty to quietly prepare myself for these evening presentations.

I can still see my companions, worn out after having worked outdoors in temperatures dropping as low as minus forty-five degrees, packed together underneath portraits of Marx, Engels, and Lenin, listening intently to lectures on themes very far removed from the reality we faced at that time.

I thought then with emotion about Proust, in his overheated cork-lined room, who would certainly have been amazed and maybe even touched to learn that, twenty years after his death, some Polish prisoners, following a whole day spent in the snow and cold, would be listening with keen interest to the story of the Duchesse de Guermantes, the death of Bergotte, and anything else I could bring myself to recall of his world of precious psychological discovery and literary beauty.

I offer here my thanks to two friends, Lieutenant Władisław Cichy, today the editor of the Polish version of *Parade* in Cairo, and Lieutenant Imek* Kohn, a medical officer with our army on the Italian front. It is to them that I dictated this essay in our cold and rank-smelling mess hall at the Gryazovets camp.

The joy of participating in an intellectual undertaking that gave us proof that we were still capable of thinking and reacting to matters of the mind—things then bearing no

*Joachim.

connection to our present reality—cast a rose-colored light on those hours spent in the former convent's dining hall, that strangest of schoolrooms, where a world we had feared lost to us forever was revived.

It was incomprehensible to us why we alone, four hundred officers and soldiers, were saved out of fifteen thousand comrades who disappeared without a trace somewhere beyond the Arctic Circle, within the confines of Siberia. From those gloomy depths, the hours spent with memories of Proust, Delacroix, Degas seemed to me among the happiest of hours.

This essay is but a humble tribute of gratitude to the French art that helped us live through those few years in the USSR.

1944

Ce n'est qu'en l'année 1924 qu'un volume de Proust me tomba dans les
mains. Fraîchement venu à Paris, connaissant de la littérature française à peine plus que des romans de second ordre dans le genre de
Farrère ou Loti, admirant au-dessus de tout un écrivain si peu "unique" du point de vue de son style, si peu typique du point de vue de
la langue française *que* comme Romain Rolland, j'essayais de m'orienter
dans la littérature moderne du pays .

C'était le temps du grand succès du "Bal du Comte d'Orgel"
ce court roman à "La Princesse de Clèves", le temps de la célébrité
montante de Cocteau, Cendrars, Morand, de la phrase télégraphique de la
brièveté et de la sècheresse voulue du style. Voilà ce qu'un étranger
voyait alors à la surface des lettres françaises.

Mais c'est alors aussi que Stock rééditait" La femme pauvre"
et les autres romans méconnus de Bloie, la N.R.F. et les oeuvres de
Charles Péguy. C'était en même temps que paraissaient les gros volumes
consécutifs d'"A la recherche du temps perdu", un immense roman d'un
certain Proust couronné par l'Académie Goncourt en 1919, qui venait de
mourir.

Attiré par le clacissisme du "Bal", par cette poésie de presti-
digitateur d'un Cocteau, je découvrais en même temps avec tremblement
le monde mystérieux de Péguy dans "Jeanne d'Arc", son style étrange
avec ses retours et répétitions infinis, mais je n'arrivais pas à sur-
monter les obstacles qui me séparaient de Proust. Je m'étais mis à lire
dans un des volumes ("Du côté des Guermantes") une description d'une
réception mondaine, la description traînait quelques centaines de pages.

Je connaissais trop peu la langue française pour goûter
l'essence même de ce livre, pour apprécier sa forme rare. J'étais habitué à des livres où il se passe quelque chose, où l'action se développe
plus prestement, racontée dans un français plus courant, je ne possédais
pas de culture littéraire suffisante pour aborder ces livres si précieux
débordants et tellement en contradiction avec ce qui nous semblait
l'esprit de l'époque. Cet esprit passager qui dans la naïveté de

LOST TIME

IT WAS only in the year 1924 that a volume of Proust fell into my hands. Newly arrived in Paris, I was barely aware of French literature beyond some second-rate novels like those by Farrère or Loti. Above all I admired Romain Rolland, a very unoriginal writer from the point of view of style and an atypical one from the point of view of the French language. I tried to adjust my bearings to the modern literature of the place.

It was a time of great success for Radiguet's *Bal du Comte d'Orgel*, a novella in the style of *La Princesse de Clèves*, a time of increasing fame for Cocteau, Cendrars, and Morand, and a time for the telegraphic sentence, with its intentional brevity and dryness of style. This was what a foreigner found on the surface of French letters at the time.

But it was also the moment when Stock was reissuing *La Femme pauvre* and Bloy's other neglected novels, and *La Nouvelle Revue Française* was republishing the works of Charles Péguy. It was at this very time that the unwieldy, sequential volumes of *À la recherche du temps perdu* began to appear, a massive novel written by a certain Proust—crowned by the Académie Goncourt in 1919—who had only recently died.

Attracted by the classicism of Radiguet's *Bal*, by the poetry of the conjurer Cocteau, I discovered at this time, tremblingly, the mysterious world of Péguy's *Jeanne d'Arc*, with its odd style of infinite returns and repetition, but I was never quite able to surmount the obstacles that kept me from Proust. I started by reading the description of a high-society party in one of his volumes (*Le côté de Guermantes*?); the description dragged on for several hundred pages.

I was too little acquainted with the French language to savor the essence of this book, to appreciate its rare form. I was more used to books where something actually happens, where the action develops more nimbly and is told in a rather more up-to-date style. I didn't have sufficient literary culture to deal with these volumes, so mannered and exuberant, and so at odds with what we thought of at the time as the spirit of the age, that fleeting spirit which represented for us, in the naiveté of our youth, a new set of laws destined to endure until the end of time. Proust's lengthy sentences, with their endless asides, myriad, remote, and unexpected associations, their strange manner of treating entangled themes without any kind of hierarchy—the value of this style, with its extreme precision and richness, seemed beyond me.

Only a year later, by chance, I opened *Albertine disparue* (the penultimate volume of *À la recherche*) and all of a sudden read from the first page to the last with increasing wonder. I have to confess it was not Proust's precious content that took me in at first, but rather the subject of this volume: the despair, the forsaken lover's anguish at being abandoned by Albertine, the description of all forms of retrospective jealousy, painful memories, feverish investigations, all that psychological insight of a great writer, with its muddle of details and references that struck right at the heart of me; it was only then that I discovered the treasure of his literary form, a new apparatus with an unforeseen precision for psychological assessment, a new world of poetry. But how was one to read it all, how could one find the time to assimilate these thousands of dense pages? I only have typhoid fever to thank for rendering me so helpless over a whole summer that I was able to read his work in its entirety. I've returned to it countless times, always discovering some new emphasis, some new perspective.

Proust's literary formation, his vision of the world, developed during the years 1890–1900, and it was between the years 1904–1905 and 1923 that almost all of the writer's body of work was created.* What did these years represent in terms of artistic and literary movements in France? We should remember that the anti-naturalist manifesto of the disciples of Zola, with its reaction against naturalism penetrating even into the master's inner circle, dates from 1889. This was the time of the symbolist school with Mallarmé, professor at the lycée Proust attended, as its leader, and Maeterlinck, who gained worldwide fame. The years 1890–1900 saw the triumph of impressionism, the taste for Italian primitives thanks to Ruskin, the Wagner craze in France, the period of post-impressionist explorations that, while building on certain elements of impressionism, at the same time contradicted its strictly naturalist essence. In music, Debussy's work revealed a tendency to parallel the impressionist and post-impressionist movements in painting. Bergson, with *L'Évolution créatrice* as his crowning achievement, was teaching classes at the Collège de France and Sarah Bernhardt was at her peak in the theater. After 1900, Diaghilev's Ballets Russes came to Paris, with its revelations of Russian music and dazzling orientalist décor, Mussorgsky, Bakst, *Shéhérazade*. And finally, Maeterlinck and Debussy's *Pelléas et Mélisande* at the Opéra.

*Proust died in November 1922.

Here we find the soil in which Proust's creative sensibility took root, the artistic events that one finds assimilated and transposed in his own body of work. We have to remember that naturalism (the final stage of realism) and its opposing forces, especially symbolism, were late nineteenth-century movements extremely rich in a variety of nuances. They brushed up against one another and got entangled; only in academic books that appeared much later were these currents strictly labeled and delineated. During his lifetime, Mallarmé was linked to Goncourt, one of the founders of naturalism, and he socialized with Zola, who agreed that he would happily "make like Mallarmé" if only he had more time, which suggests that Mallarmé's poetic inspirations hardly contradicted Zola's own naturalist theories. But it was Mallarmé's close friend, the painter Degas, who best represented the highest form of entanglement, who used elements otherwise considered incompatible, who embodied the whole framework of the art of this time. Degas, passionate admirer of both Delacroix and Ingres, exhibited with the impressionists from the very start. A painter of dancers, of horse racing, of yawning laundresses holding irons in their hands, of portraits pushed to the very limit of their analysis—this naturalist par excellence was among the first to exploit the discoveries revealed in photographic snapshots and who, with his exacting and cruel eye, studied the city of Paris in its most unexplored aspects. At the same time, he fought with his friends the impressionists. He raged against their contempt for the principles and abstract rules governing classical painting—composition, surface, etc. Throughout his whole life he endeavored to unite an abstract sense of harmony and construction with the immediate sensations of reality, to bring the impressionist's discoveries in line with the classical tradition of a Poussin.

Degas also composed pure sonnets in the manner of Mallarmé, poems that Valéry admired. The hero of *À la recherche* singles out Degas as the highest authority on the art of his time.

The end of the nineteenth century, from which the Proustian vision ensues, is one of the supreme moments in the history of art. France at that time produced a number of artistic geniuses who arrived at an art of synthesis that reconciled all the profound contradictions ripping the era apart. Abstract elements were joined together with an immediate and exacting sensibility of the real world. This synthesis was the outcome of minutely analyzed personal experience; it was not a static notion derived from preconceived, second-hand ideas. But the anti-naturalist movement—represented first in literature by the symbolists, then in painting by Gauguin (*"cette sacrée nature"*)—destroyed this brief moment of richness and in 1907 led to cubism, an art opposed to any engagement with reality. Before the war, cubism yielded to the influence of the Italian futurists, with their manifestos calling for the destruction of all museums, the very sanctuaries of Proust. But by this time Proust's confinement had already become more and more established, given his personal unhappiness, his monumental labor, his illness. Obsessed by his book, he pursued his work in complete independence of the artistic currents of the day. After the war, cubism, futurism, and their spin-offs expanded victoriously into considerable spheres of influence. In self-serving, boisterous acclamation, they cleverly insisted that all other art was forever passé. Proust's novel seems at first to be a book from another world, pretentious, solidly bourgeois, tainted by an outmoded snobbery. For all these avid young people, in principle full of enthusiasm and revolution, hardly aware of the history of French literature, of the very soil of France and its huge wealth of literary tradition of which Proust's work was the fruit, for all these postwar "barbarians" flocking to Paris from the four corners of the globe, Proust was, from the start, off-putting, strange, and absolutely unacceptable.

I

EVERY great book is profoundly tied in one way or another to the very matter of the life of its author. But this link is even more pronounced and perhaps more integral to the work of Proust. The very theme of *À la recherche* is Proust's life, transposed; the principal character writes in the first person, and page after page reads like a barely concealed confession. Through the book's principal hero we encounter a grandmother, adoring and caring for her only grandson, unmistakably recalling traits of Proust's mother; we find Baron de Charlus, whose prototype is Baron de Montesquiou,* one of the most highly visible aristocrats in high society at that time, known for his splendor and originality. Not a chronicle of the world in 1900, the entire work represents this world reconceived and transposed. Like Proust, the hero of his book is sickly, he lives in the same milieu as Proust and suffers from creative impotence much as young Proust did. The hero has the author's temperament and hypersensitivity, and, like Proust, the hero's great misfortune is to lose his grandmother (for Proust it was the death of his mother). The ensuing heartbreak produces the same result— a feeling of unreality, and the awareness that the pleasures

*Montesquiou was a count, not a baron.

of life and a final understanding of it exist in the act of creation, the sole true life and true reality.

His friends saw him as a fully realized writer, a mature man; the most perceptive of them already suspected his greatness and his genius. (The finest tributes to Proust appear in *Hommage à Proust*, from *La Nouvelle Revue Française* in 1924–26,* with articles by Mauriac, Cocteau, Gide, Fernandez, Lenormand, etc. The most vivid and poignant descriptions of Proust that I know are by Léon-Paul Fargue; there are more which I don't recall.)

Still a young man, Proust had begun to frequent the most elegant and fashionable Parisian salons. Madame Straus, née Halévy, one of the wittiest of the society women of the French upper bourgeoisie, called him her "little page boy." An eighteen-year-old youth with beautiful black eyes, Proust sat on an ottoman at her feet during her weekly gatherings. He became a habitué at the home of Madame Caillavet and Anatole France, where he met everyone who was anyone in the political and literary world at that time. He even managed to insinuate himself within the most exclusive circles of the Faubourg Saint-Germain.

In his early twenties, Proust understood that the illness he had developed during his childhood was incurable. He acknowledged this and organized his life accordingly, accepting his illness as a necessary evil. Only after his death would many of his friends understand the degree to which Proust had been really ill and how great a toll this had taken on his spirit and youthfulness during those outings when

---

* The exact reference is: *Hommage à Marcel Proust*, Paris, Gallimard, 1927. *Les Cahiers Marcel Proust*, volume 1.

his health allowed him a few days or a week or two of respite.

As he aged, Proust became increasingly intolerant of any fragrance or perfume. "Leave at once and toss your handkerchief out at the door," he ordered anyone who dropped in by chance wearing a scented handkerchief in their pockets. One spring day, the author of memorable passages on apple trees in bloom wanted to see an orchard once more. He decided to make a trip outside Paris in a closed car, and only by keeping the windows shut was he able to admire his beloved trees in bloom. Buried in his work, he found the slightest noise untenable. Proust spent his final long years of labor in a cork-lined room, stretched out on a bed beside a piano, the piano piled high with a mountain of books. Medicine bottles littered his night table along with sheets of paper covered in his nervous handwriting. He would write in the most awkward position imaginable, lying in bed, propped up on his right elbow, as he himself claimed in his letters, "writing for me is an agony."

I've already mentioned the considerable role Proust's mother played in this life of chronic illness. She adored him, looked after him, almost never left his side. Proust, with his feminine nature, inhaled her inimitable and intelligent tenderness right up until her death. Frequently overcome by sentimental, intellectual, and artistic passions, he might occasionally have forgotten the degree to which she was indispensable to him. Despite everything, she believed in his talent, in his genius, even as his young friends dismissed him as a snob and a loser, and while his robust, realistic father saw in his son's behavior only an aggravating slothfulness that would lead nowhere in terms of finding a career. Into the relationship between the novel's protagonist and his grandmother, Proust poured all his love for his own mother, his youthful egoism, his periodic inability to understand to what degree his mother's (in the novel his grandmother's) love for him was absolute, selfless, and sublime. The cold precision with which, in imperceptible little ways, he exposed the cruelty of his early years, his own cruelty, well after his mother's death, is another proof of the extent to which the writer, as his own analyst, was free of all human *amour-propre*, of all desire to embellish himself or to retouch his portrait slightly. Take as an example how the young hero of the novel, a boy of fifteen or sixteen, spends his afternoons in the gardens of the Champs-Élysées, where he meets a young girl, Gilberte (the daughter of Odette, Swann's former mistress, after Jeanne). At dinner one night he is consumed with impatience, champing at the bit to leave for the Champs-Élysées with an intensity comparable to the anguish of his younger self years earlier at the old house in the country as he waited for the arrival of his mother and her goodnight kiss. The hero's grandmother, already ill by then, is long delayed coming back from her daily outing in a carriage before dinner. The boy notices his first reaction: "Perhaps Grandmother has had another attack, perhaps she's already dead, and I'll be late for my rendezvous on the Champs-Élysées." To this he adds, with similar distancing objectivity and so-called indifference: "When one loves someone, one loves no one else." Innumerable touches of this kind deepen the light and shadow of filial affection and motherly love, bearing the imprint of intimate personal experience.

Proust's mother died around 1904 or 1905.* This was his

---

*She died in 1905.

first great calamity, the first heartbreak Proust lived through. His whole anxious, unfulfilled, chaotic life in society—the part of his life that made work impossible, that aggravated his sickly condition, that had made his mother suffer so, however silently—broke apart. Battered by grief, Proust withdrew from his society friends for a long time. It was then that his mother's dream of seeing him become a writer began to haunt him in a decisive and concrete way. Having behind him only some society-page articles and a few other visionary pages written as a very young man ("La Route des peupliers vue de voiture"* and *Les Plaisirs et les jours*, ignored by all at the time), he still felt incapable of beginning the great work he already felt forming within himself.

Another literary project presented itself, not just a passing enthusiasm, as a way to make progress, and so Proust began to labor on something that required he get to work every day, a hard pill for him to swallow. He began translating the complete works of Ruskin, who had had an enormous aesthetic influence on Proust's generation. In the years 1890–1900, the rediscovery of the art of the Italian primitives, the cult of Venice, and the adoration of Botticelli all stemmed from Ruskin's writings. Proust prefaced his translation of Ruskin with a massive introduction. This work marks Proust's entry into the second phase of his life, colored by the same passion, the same lack of moderation one found in his social and sentimental life. He flung himself into his literary work. From this time forward, until his death, he isolated himself more and more in his cork-lined room. Proust would still be seen at very late hours, at parties or at the Ritz, but these

*This article appeared in *Le Figaro* in 1907 under the title "Impressions de route en automobile." Proust later reprinted it as "Journées en automobile" in *Pastiches et mélanges* (1919).

were only spontaneous outings in which he sought to clarify and to verify, to "botanize" for his immense new *Comédie Humaine.*

The slow and painful transformation of a passionate and narrowly egotistical being into a man who gives himself over wholly to some great work or other that devours him, destroys him, lives in his blood, is a trial every creative being must endure. *"Si le grain ne meurt..."* If we're speaking about creative artists, this transformation comes to each one differently, more or less self-consciously, almost conventionally. Goethe said that in the life of a creative man, biography can and must be considered only up to the thirty-fifth year, after that it's no longer his life story, but his struggle with the substance of his work that must become central and, more and more, increasingly absorbing.* But rarely is this division between the two halves of a creative man so clearly demarcated. Conrad—who, at thirty-six, put sailing behind him completely, abandoned the sea in order to embark upon the immense labor needed for his literary undertaking—seems to me to offer certain analogies. Corot, on the other hand, strikes us as an artist free from drama or struggle. According to this provincial draper's son, with his dull and conventional biography, only art was ever his mistress. Naturally I'm simplifying a good deal so as not to stray too far. Nevertheless, I think I'm hardly betraying Corot by affirming that the

---

*[*Czapski's note*] I'm quoting Goethe here from memory, perhaps distorting his text. Rozanov, attacked by critics for imprecise or distorted citations, quipped: "There's nothing easier than to quote a text precisely, you just have to check the books. It's far more difficult to assimilate a quotation to the point where it becomes yours and becomes part of you." If I misquote it's precisely because of the impossibility of checking in books. Also, I possess neither Rozanov's glibness nor his entitlement as a writer of genius.

extreme harmony and sweetness of his work, with its gemlike quality and balance (thanks to which it avoided all the extremes of time and place), appears to me profoundly tied to his attitude towards life.

How ridiculous remarks made by Proust scholars and superficial readers about Proust's snobbism seem! What meaning can this word possibly have in respect to a writer of his stature who observes the fashionable world with such lucidity and distance?

Proust lived more and more by night. Year after year his health deteriorated. Among all his other strange symptoms, he always felt like he was freezing. He had all his evening dress shirts lined. These shirts were all covered with brown burned spots because he liked to warm them before putting them on, but would hold them too close to the flame. From time to time Proust could be found at the most exclusive salons, where he had once been a familiar figure. He always arrived just as a party was beginning to break up, but he would manage, more brilliantly than ever, to take everyone's breath away with his animated talk, keeping everyone spellbound until dawn. He could also be found at the Ritz Hotel at impossible hours in the center of a group of extravagant Parisian revelers.

Apart from these rare escapades, he hardly ever went out. More and more, he lost all sense of time. War broke out. Naturally, mobilizing the gravely ill Proust was out of the question. But Proust, a hothouse flower living under the free and unbureaucratic regime of the pre-1914 French government, had no idea of the formalities each citizen must submit to in wartime; he lived in great fear that some failing or another on his part would compromise him before the military authorities. Suddenly, he received a summons to appear before the draft board. He made a muddle of the time, couldn't sleep at all, stuffed himself with pills, then presented himself at staff headquarters at two o'clock in the morning. He returned home, extremely surprised to have found the office closed.

After the war, in the final years of his life, the Duchesse de Clermont-Tonnerre secured a box at the Opéra for a large charity event with the idea of allowing Proust to observe once again the society from which the vigor of his great work was drawn. Proust arrived late, seated himself in a corner of the box, turned his back to the stage and never stopped talking. The next day the duchess remarked to him that it had hardly been worth the bother of taking a box to help him venture out if he had had no intention of paying attention to what was going on. With a sly smile, Proust proceeded to recount, with meticulous precision, everything that had occurred in the theater and on the stage, piling up a wealth of details that no one else had noticed, and then added: "Don't worry, when it comes to my work, *I'm busy as a bee.*"

Proust's sensibility was only fully realized in his literary work. He had a way of taking in events with a complex, delayed reaction. Visiting the Louvre, for example, he would see everything but respond to nothing. Only later, at night, lying in bed, he would be consumed by attacks of real fever brought on by excitement. All the unhappiness of Proust's sentimental life, all the petty and cruel heartbreak that provoked his sensibility—causing him to react far more strongly than his friends, in a different way, and at a different time—served him above all to recreate in solitude the world of lived experiences, recasting them and transposing them in *À la recherche*.

From early youth, Proust was aware of his vocation. He

saw his duty not in an immediate discharge of enthusiasm whenever touched by some impression at the moment it was happening, but rather in the effort made to plumb its depths, to clarify it, to get to the source of the impression and render it consciously. He told a story about himself as a young boy, enraptured by the reflection of a beam of sunlight on a pond, beating his umbrella against the ground, crying, "*Zut! Zut! Zut!*" He was already aware of feeling that he lacked a primary capacity—not to immediately externalize an impression, but to deepen it. In *Le Temps retrouvé*, Proust mocks enthusiasts overcome by music, incapable of refraining from making overwrought gestures that expressed their admiration. "Oh my lord, gadzooks, I've never heard anything so beautiful!"

Several points of departure in Proust's work give us insight into his creative process, several visionary pages that have already become classic. These concern the madeleine in the first part of *Du côté de chez Swann* and the uneven paving stones in the last part of *Le Temps retrouvé*. The ailing hero is having a cup of tea and moistens some little morsels of madeleine in it. The taste of this tea-dampened pastry brings forth his childhood, when he used to eat madeleines in the same way. It is not an intentional or chronological memory of his childhood but an involuntary evocation that emerges from the cup of tea flavored by the madeleine. (Proust repeatedly insists that only involuntary memory is significant in art.) Like the little pieces of Japanese paper (Proust's metaphor) which, thrown into a bowl, swell up, expand, and take on the form of flowers, of houses or faces, the memory released by the fragrance of the madeleine rises, deepens, and, bit by bit, takes on the shape of his childhood home, the old gothic church and the countryside of his youth, the faces of his old aunts, Françoise the cook, Swann, a frequent visitor to the house, and the faces of his mother and grandmother, adored above all others. This tiny impression at the outset announces the whole work.

Another point in his work provides a key not only to Proust's creative process, but to his biography. It seems to us a barely disguised confession, a precise revelation of his vocation, one lived by the author himself and retold as the hero's revelation. Exhausted by his futile efforts to become a writer, following years of agonized indecision, of continual sacrifice and unfulfilled pleasure, of superficial friendships and relationships, the hero (or Proust himself) decides to give it all up. He's no writer. He has no talent, that was just an illusion; he's no longer young and the time has come to admit it. Conclusion: if his vocation as a writer was only a dream, he must accept that and devote himself, for the rest of his life, finally with no qualms or remorse, to his friends, to his enjoyable society acquaintances. In this completely new frame of mind, resigned and relaxed, Proust* makes his way to the Hôtel de Guermantes for an elegant reception. At the very moment he passes under the archway in the courtyard, he must step aside to let an automobile pass; his feet land on two paving stones that are uneven. At this most unexpected moment, the author recalls having felt the same sensation of two identically uneven paving stones under his feet years ago in Venice, in Saint Mark's Square, and all at once he has a clear and electrifying vision of Venice and all that he saw and experienced there. He has the sudden conviction of a book existing within him, with all its details, only waiting to be realized.

Struck dumb by this revelation when he least expected

*Actually the novel's hero.

such a thing, Proust enters the reception hall of the Guermantes. He is seeing it for the first time since the end of the
war, and is made welcome by a butler who has known him
for many years, who shows such unexpected respect that
Proust realizes he has ceased to be a young man. In a small
antechamber, he sits and waits for an intermission in the
concert taking place in the principal ballroom. He is served
a glass of tea with a heavily starched napkin. Contact with
this napkin prompts a memory in him, no less clear and
precise, of another napkin with the identical sensation (shock,
commotion) from many years before, at the seashore, in the
Grand Hôtel at Balbec, a revelation no less precise and no
less lightning-like than those of Venice.

The hero, who had set out for the Hôtel de Guermantes
convinced of having broken with his literary ambitions once
and for all, spends the hours of his visit in a state of feverish
clarity, acknowledging the certainty that this vocation will
completely uproot his life. He observes the assembled group
of friends from his earlier life, already deformed by age,
growing older, bloated or withering away, and then sees
young people there emerging among them, a new generation
who seem to harbor so poignantly the same hopes his old or
dead friends once held. All this he sees with new eyes, lucidly,
detached, and from a distance; finally, he knows what he is
meant to do with his life. It's he, and he alone in this crowd,
who will make them all come to life again, he knows it with
a force of certainty that death has become a matter of indifference to him. On his way home, dreaming of a new life of
hard work and fulfillment, the idea occurs to him suddenly
that he might be run over by the first streetcar, and this
seems to him a horrible prospect. We know now that the
major part of Proust's final volume, which appeared in print

only after his death, without his final editing of the text, had been written before all the others, giving us proof again that the crowning achievement of his novel, its conclusion, was both a personal confession and a starting point.

2

I'M AWARE that in speaking about Proust, I'm filling my talk with details of his work and his personal life, but I haven't yet managed to express, even less to elucidate for myself, what exactly the novelty, the discovery, and the essence of his work consists of. Without a single book in hand, and more to the point, in possession of virtually no philosophical learning, I'm hardly in a position to touch upon this critical problem. It's impossible to speak deeply about Proust if one detaches him from the philosophical currents of his time, or remains silent about the philosophy of Bergson, his contemporary, who played such a large role in his intellectual development. Proust attended Bergson's classes, which enjoyed a great popularity between 1890–1900, and as far as I recall, he knew the man personally.* Even the title of his opus shows us how preoccupied Proust was by the question of time, and time, seen from a philosophical point of view, was the focus of Bergson's work. I've read plenty of studies about the question of time in Proust's work. To be fully honest, I can only recall the repeated affirmations of Proust's originality in this field, yet the principal thesis of Bergson's philosophy must once again be acknowledged. Bergson insisted that life is continuous and our perception

*Bergson was married to Proust's cousin.

of it discontinuous. It follows that our intelligence is incapable of forming an adequate idea of life. It is not intelligence but intuition that provides us with an adequate idea of life. (Intuition in humans corresponds to instinct in animals.) Proust attempts to overcome the problem of the discontinuity of perception with involuntary memory, with the intuition of creating a new form and a new vision that can furnish us with an impression of life's continuity.

Today we call all immense novels, more or less influenced by Proust's form, "romans-fleuves." Yet none of these books is as worthy of such a designation as *À la recherche du temps perdu*. I'll try to explain by making a comparison. It's not what the stream is carrying along with it—branches, a corpse, some pearls—that represents the particular direction of the stream, but the current itself, continuous and without end. The reader of Proust, slipping along on an apparently monotonous tide, is not struck by plot, but by some character or other, by the wave's ceaseless motion, as of life itself. The rudimentary design Proust had in mind for his novel couldn't be realized in the form he had hoped for. He had wanted the whole thing to appear in a single volume, without paragraphs, without margins, without sections or chapters. The prospect was seen as completely ridiculous by the most refined editors in Paris, and as a result Proust was forced to break his book up into fifteen or sixteen sections, as each separately titled volume was broken down into two or three sections. However, Proust still managed to force the hand of his editors and succeeded in creating something new, at least from the point of view of the form of the modern novel. No single part of his book represents a unified whole in itself when detached from the others. Breaks in the text seem willfully unjustifiable, determined by page count rather than by the development of any one theme or another. It must be added that his themes were so absolutely entangled that it was impossible to make a clean break appear as anything other than a question of practical necessity. The volumes were produced in extremely small and compact print runs, with narrow margins and no paragraph breaks. Only a handful of chapters show any logical harmony as far as a breakdown into individual sections is concerned. By this unusual manner of printing, Proust managed to accentuate both the continuity and the unfinishedness of the stream of his work.

Proust's sentences upended modern norms of brevity and concision. Immensely long, they could go on for a page and a half, printed in this compact manner with no paragraph breaks. His sentences were seen as grotesque by admirers of "the French style," who insisted on the old cliché of necessarily short and clear sentences. A sentence by Proust was, on the contrary, tangled and full of parenthetical asides, with parentheses inside parentheses, with the most disparate associations spreading out in every direction and metaphors dragging along towards new parentheses and new associations. Proust was attacked: his style was not French, but German. The great German critic Curtius, an admirer, also pointed out a Germanic element in the Proustian sentence. Proust's reaction to this thesis is noteworthy, as is his vast literary culture. He claimed that any kinship between his sentences and German sentences was neither accidental nor a sign of weakness, but rather a reflection of the fact that contemporary German sentences most resembled Latin sentences. It wasn't German but the French language of the sixteenth century, much more closely aligned with Latin, that his style resembled. And, he added, the celebrated clarity and brevity of "the French style" was a relatively new development. It stemmed from the Encyclopedist and rationalist eighteenth century, when the French language was more steeped in conversation than in literature. German, essentially a written language, developed in many locations. French, on the other hand, was polished in a single place, in Paris, which, as Goethe had already observed, served to centralize all information and created, thanks to this, a unique intellectual climate.

Boy-Żeleński, translator of Proust into Polish, managed to translate more than half of Proust's work before the war began in 1939. While many of his pages constitute a masterpiece of Polish literature, his translation departs still further from Proust's original plan. On account of this I had a talk with Boy in which he defended his position, claiming that he didn't set out from a position of working *against* Proust but *for* him; it was always his intention to clarify the Proustian text. Boy knew Proust wanted to be a popular success. It's wrong to sanctify a writer—one has to edit him in a manner that makes him most readable. Anyway, Proust had consented to alter his original idea of a single volume in France. When it came to a Polish version, Boy insisted, Proust's extended sentences were unacceptable, beyond the means of the Polish language, which must resort to the use of the words "*który, która*" (the Polish equivalent for *que*) over and over again. But Boy pushed his translation even further, making the Polish version appear in a far more readable form, with paragraphs, with dialogue separated out line by line, no longer jumbled in the body of the text. He doubled the number of the original volumes. "I sacrificed the precious for the sake of the essential," he declared. The immediate result was that suddenly Proust read very easily.

From the moment his Polish translation appeared, people in Warsaw loved to repeat the joke that the French should just translate Proust back into French from the Polish translation; then at last he would become hugely popular in France.

In speaking about Proust's style, one must emphasize its quality of preciousness. The pages sparkle and shine with riches of metaphoric language, exotic and precious associations. These riches never become an end in themselves. They only serve to deepen, to render the masterful ideas in his sentences more palpably, with more freshness. We mustn't forget that Proust's literary debut coincided with the cult of Mallarmé, that he was an admirer of this poet's work. He savored all the delicacy, all the original ideas of the French language of the period, from Baudelaire and the Parnassians to the symbolists in poetry, from the Goncourt brothers to Villiers de l'Isle-Adam and Anatole France in prose. Much as he admired modern literature, Proust knew even more about the history of French literature. He'd had an exceptional literary education and possessed a staggering memory. Friends boasted that Proust could declaim whole pages of Balzac by heart. And not only Balzac, who seems to be his most immediate precursor and to whom he owed the most, but whole pages of Saint-Simon, whose work he also admired and knew deeply. And plenty of others.

Proust left behind several pastiches. I remember a sendup of Balzac. In this parody, surprising in its accuracy and good humor, Proust exaggerated Balzac's pompous and superlative descriptions of duchesses and countesses—pure as angels, noble, gorgeous as goddesses or cunning as Satan. I have a vague recollection that Proust maintained that the best way to free oneself from the power of another writer's influence was to set out and write a pastiche. When one considers the value Proust put on every word, it's worth noting how this always ailing man, who was thought of as superficial, worked so rigorously on his style. Some small examples: late one night, as Paris was completely plunged in darkness, the critic Ramon Fernandez was awakened by an unexpected visit from Proust. "Pardon me, I've only come to ask a small favor of you. Please repeat for me in Italian these two words: *senza rigore.*" Fluent in Italian, Fernandez obliged, repeating the two words. Proust vanished as quickly as he had appeared. "I was so moved," Fernandez recounted much later, after Proust's death, "when I read in one of his volumes a conversation with Albertine in which motoring is discussed and where she utters these two very words in passing. While composing that page, Proust had needed not only to know the meaning of these two foreign words, but to hear them spoken by someone who knew Italian well."*

In an edition of Proust's letters, I found a short note, dating from the end of his life, to a Parisian critic he had wanted to meet (I think Boulenger) because of an enthusiastic article the critic had written about his work. In his postscript Proust wrote, "Please forgive my using the word *que* twice, but I'm in a terrible hurry." I see some of my listeners smile. Anyway, this relentless honesty, this cult of good form and attention to the least detail, rewards us with writers of the stature of Flaubert or Proust. And it is the lack of awareness among us of the seriousness of this effort, pushed to the extreme, that has destroyed many great talents.

Here's another commonplace about Proust's work to which even I often subscribe: Proust is naturalism as if seen through

---

*In the typescripts, these two words appear as *senza vigore*. See "Fernandez" in the glossary.

a microscope. But the more I consider this, the more misguided it seems to me. It's not the microscope that reveals to us the secret of Proust, but another aspect of his talent. I'll try to render this intelligibly by means of a comparison. In *Du côté de chez Swann*, Proust tells how his grandmother always gave him gifts representing some memento of a work of art passed through several artistic filters. The novel's young protagonist dreams of going to Venice and is meant to travel there with his parents, but an illness prevents the journey from taking place. His grandmother doesn't then give him a photograph of Saint Mark's Basilica or some other Venetian masterpiece, rather she gives him a painting of such a masterpiece—and again, not just a simple photograph of this painting, but an engraving of it made by another eminent artist. For Proust, a fact is never a simple fact. From the very beginning, it is infinitely enriched and transposed in his brain by the vision of an artist separated from the world by illness, by cork walls, by a brain steeped in literature, by artistic and scientific associations. But what most contradicts this idea of the "microscope" (histology) is that Proust's interconnections are immensely divergent, drawn from all times, from all the arts, so that Proust's pages become much more an account of his own thoughts awakened by a collision with a fact, rather than just the facts themselves.

I recently reread the beginning of *War and Peace*. It begins with a twenty-two page description of a ball given by Anna Pavlovna Scherer, a lady-in-waiting to the emperor's mother. In a masterly fashion, Tolstoy describes for us the atmosphere, the intrigues hidden beneath the compliments, and we make the acquaintance in a definitive and palpable manner of the whole aristocratic world invited by Anna Pavlovna. The first chapter, barely two pages long, a masterpiece of subtlety, consists of a conversation between Prince Vassily and the hostess. Their exchange reveals a mutual cunning that provides us with a colorful glimpse into the manner of expression used in such places at that time. In Proust's volumes *Le Côté de Guermantes* and *Sodome et Gomorrhe*, we encounter fundamentally the same theme at heart, but with the difference that a simple tea with a duchess can fill a thick volume; the description of a conversation such as Anna Pavlovna has in *War and Peace* provides Proust with a pretext for filling tens, even hundreds of crammed pages. This is not simply a microscopic analysis of each wrinkle, of each gesture, of each fragrance, it's also a vast web of associations that leads to other associations, the most unexpected and the most remote in time, to metaphors that each time open for us new vistas onto still other metaphors.

It would be absurd to speak of "formalism" or pure form in the case of Proust. To begin with, there is no such thing as pure formalism in great literature. A new form, nothing artificial but something alive, cannot exist without new content. In Proust's work we feel an endless search, a passionate desire to render clearly and legibly the awareness of a whole world of impressions and connections, the most difficult to attain. The form of the novel, the construction of a sentence, all the metaphors and associations are an internal necessity, reflecting the very essence of his vision. It's not the simple fact that haunts Proust, as I've said, but the secret laws that govern facts, it's the desire to make us aware of the least discernible secret workings of being.

3

I'VE ALREADY mentioned that only the first volumes of *À la recherche*, those that make up *Du côté de chez Swann*, were published before the war. They were the only volumes untouched by the evolution and changes in composition produced by Proust's labor during the long war years. It is also the most precise and sharply focused part of the novel. *Du côté de chez Swann* already contains the first variations on all the motifs that make up the fabric of the volumes that follow. The ensuing volumes, which contain all the new material brought forth during the war, the new impressions and considerations, the huge expansion and essential reworking, were, nevertheless, only a further development of what had already been set into motion in *Du côté de chez Swann*. Let's have a look at the basic themes: provincial France and the reclusive life of his retired old aunts; an ancient gothic church; descriptions of the countryside that have become classics in world literature; and Françoise, the old servant whom we meet in all the volumes, who, in the cast of characters of *À la recherche*, represents the rustic, working-class element. These are the first themes. Next comes childhood and the dramas of childhood: filial love and maternal love. The relationships between the hero and his mother and his grandmother become principal themes. The young boy's visits to church each Sunday—the stained glass windows showing members of the Guermantes dynasty as knights at the time of the Crusades, and the contemplation of the current Duchesse de Guermantes in flesh and blood—spark his passionate interest in the Faubourg Saint-Germain, a subject he continues to study and analyze throughout all the volumes to come. We meet Swann in the first section, and almost the whole of the second section is filled with the love story of Swann and Odette, a young woman of the demimonde. This Odette, the personification of a woman who lives solely to be loved by men, unleashes mad passion, much suffering, and insane jealousy in Swann (a theme Proust studies very thoroughly and to which he devotes hundreds of pages in *Du côté de chez Swann* and also later in *Albertine** and *Albertine disparue*). Thanks to Swann we gain access to the world of the wealthy Parisian bourgeoisie, in the salon of Madame Verdurin, a model of bourgeois wealth, a social climber, and a snob.

The hero's childhood, the shocks and wounds that determine the course of his life, and the development of his moral and physical being are the central themes of *Du côté de chez Swann*. In speaking of it, I'd like to touch lightly on a seminal episode in the later life of the author. The child, who goes on to become a young man, who grows into the mature man that Proust calls "I," spends his summers with his parents in a small provincial village. The first cruel sufferings he recalls occur while he is in bed, having been sent upstairs from the dinner table to go to sleep, as he impatiently and anxiously waits for his mother's goodnight kiss. His mother doesn't always come upstairs to kiss him goodnight. Dinner

---

* Throughout his talks, Czapski consistently refers to Proust's fifth volume, *La Prisonnière*, as *Albertine*.

carries on longer than usual. The child's father sees in his wife's obligatory visits to their overly sensitive son an exaggerated sentimentality, undesirable from the point of view of child-rearing. One night the boy can contain himself no longer. Seeing that it is unlikely his mother will come, he surmounts his fear of his father, jumps barefoot out of bed, and waits, fragile and sick as he is, for a quarter of an hour at the top of the dark stairs until his mother makes her way upstairs to go to her room and to bed. You can imagine the fright he feels when he sees his mother coming up followed by his father, carrying a lamp in one hand. Fearing the worst, his mother makes desperate gestures for her child to flee, but his father has already noticed his presence. But instead of any paternal thunder, he reacts in an unexpected way, revealing the inconsistency of a grown person's relative indifference to a child's pressing and dramatic reality. "But what a state this boy is in! Go with him quickly," he says to his wife, "and spend the night in his room." The boy, who had counted on the worst response to his hysterical insubordination, receives quite the opposite from his father, on the contrary, he's granted the realization of a longstanding dream of spending a whole night not by himself but being lulled to sleep by his mother, as she reads aloud to him from his favorite book. In a stunning categorical assertion, the writer adds that his father's inconsistency on this evening was the starting point for all his future physical and psychic maladies: his nervous sickness, his inability to contain himself in the face of his desires, his complicated symptoms with their roots steeped in his nervous weakness, all stem from that night.

No less essential in the study of Proust, for the hero's biography and that of Proust himself, is the second section of *Du côté de chez Swann*, whose pages are filled almost exclusively with an analysis of Swann and his love for Odette. This character represents a transposition of Proust himself and a certain man named Haas. A wealthy man of Jewish origins belonging to the generation of Proust's parents, Haas was, in the 1870s, one of the most elegant of Parisians—a member of the Jockey Club, friend of the Prince of Wales, of Prince Sagan, etc. Swann, like Haas, is a refined and intelligent man of the world, whose essential, natural charm rests in a rational and smooth egoism, a man for whom neither money nor high society represents an end in itself but solely a means to bring him into the circles where he can most be himself. He's a man capable of rejecting his social position with a simple gesture (which, for a Jewish bourgeois of the 1890s, was an unprecedented accomplishment) as soon as he encounters the absolute and tormenting love which undoes him completely. Odette, former cocotte—her love affairs, her secret life, their natural, sincere, and passionate love—is but a brief entry point into the breakdown of that love, a world where Swann realizes plainly and painfully that his passion for this woman only exists when she is separated from him. I don't think in all of world literature there exists a more detailed analysis of this theme, nothing more exacting or insightful that compares with these unforgettable pages of Proust. I want to tell you about a small incident, an incident that has already become classic and that I keep vividly in my memory. Odette becomes secretive, and over a period of months, Swann, using all his psychological wiles and all his wealth, is unable to discover whether she is betraying him or with whom. But a gradual estrangement is clear. Around the edges of this period in their relationship, Proust adds a perceptive remark. We can never know what makes an abandoned lover suffer most: verifiable betrayals, numerous lovers, a single lover she prefers to him, or an entirely harmless pastime that proves above all that the estrangement has become definitive.

Proust describes Odette's days spent without Swann, even though several weeks earlier she had been incapable of spending a whole day away from him. She has no lover and drags herself around idly, sitting in restaurants or cafés, bored with everything. But she prefers all this to meeting up with Swann, who is suffering fatally, martyring himself to nostalgia, barely able to detect where she has been spending her time, intercepting signals from her that suggest different and unexpected places. His jealousy and suffering create a world of suppositions that misinterpret her inclination to roam about. Yet Swann's misery would have been even more profound were he to learn that she was leaving him for no one else, that she preferred boredom and solitude to his love. It's this very love of Swann's that, above all, inspires Proust to write his most unforgettable pages in one of the following volumes.

For many months Odette avoids Swann. He no longer sees her. She's merely an incredibly painful memory he can't get rid of, rendering him absolutely incapable of any kind of activity or interest. One day he tries to rouse himself from his torpor and decides to attend a reception at the home of the Comtesse de Saint-Euverte. How such a gathering would have amused him before he met Odette! How much all the members of the upper crust who adore him begrudge Swann his preference for a tart, a woman of no position, to their company. And how pointedly this society keeps reminding him of it. Perhaps, Swann thinks, he'll find a few hours of forgetfulness. The description of this party is perfectly characteristic of Proust, with its richness of character types, packed with innumerable associations; he compares the

brilliantly costumed footmen to figures in a Botticelli painting, describes the inimitable style of the Duchesse de Guermantes through snippets of her conversation, and exposes
the anti-Semitism, rather fashionable at the time, of a second-
rate countess, expressed in her surprise at finding Swann
being received in the salon of a hostess who has bishops in
her family. Swann returns to this world as an old habitué,
warmly received by the most dazzling women of the era. But
only an old general arouses his attention, unexpectedly, a
general writing a treatise on a military leader of France. The
cause of Swann's interest? The street bearing this military
leader's name is the street where Odette lives.

A concert begins and all of a sudden the orchestra is playing the sonata by Vinteuil. The principal motif for violin is
the music that above all things in the world reminds Swann
of the happiest hours of his love. He first heard this music
and discovered it to be a modern work of exceptional beauty
at gatherings at Madame Verdurin's, where Swann had gone
on a regular basis to pass his evenings. His admiration for
Vinteuil was known to the regulars of the Verdurin salon,
and the motif was repeatedly played in order to please him.
Listening to this exceptional music while seated beside Odette,
filled with love for her, he so entwined these two sensations
that now, as the violin is being played for this indifferent,
sophisticated crowd, the motif offers concrete proof of his
past happiness, just what he had been trying to escape. It
overcomes him like a physical, wrenching pain in his heart,
reliving this happiness, lost forever. Swann, worldly, supremely
reserved, knowing how to hide any intimate emotionality
under a mask of indifference, is incapable of holding back
his tears. A precise description, perhaps Proust's most difficult and affecting, appears in the following pages: that of

the music itself, as the same motif pours forth miraculously from the violin's sound box, freshly reopening the barely healed scar on Swann's painful wound at the depth of his being. The sonata ends; the person sitting beside Swann, some countess or other, exclaims: "I've never heard anything so sublime. That sonata has moved me beyond anything else." But, overwhelmed by a fit of affectation, she adds under her breath, "Except for a séance."

4

IN THE volumes that follow *Du côté de chez Swann*, we encounter again the development and extreme interweaving of themes that began there. I'll limit myself to a few psychological problems described by Proust that are fixed in my memory more vividly than others and recount just a few scenes. I'm not making the case that the pages I speak about are the most valuable, it's just a hierarchy subjectively fixed by my enthusiasm. I can't recall ever having gone back to Proust—and I've done that many times—without discovering some new emphasis, some new insight each time. I've already spoken about the grandmother to you. It is the death of this woman, beloved by the hero above all others—whose memory will not leave him until his own death—which binds the hero to what Proust calls intermittencies of the heart. (This phrase, now classic, is known today even by people who have not yet dared to read the huge novel.)

The grandmother dies of uremia. Only some pages in Tolstoy can compare with these pages describing the death of a person who was, undoubtedly, a close transposition of Proust's own mother: the gradual breakdown of consciousness of the loved one on the threshold of death, the reactions of everyone close to her, beginning with the hero's mother, mute and heartbroken with sadness, and moving on to Françoise, whose intense loyalty is coupled with a nearly brutal attitude towards death. She forcibly combs the grandmother's hair, then sits her down before a mirror to take in her ravaged face, filling her with terror and shattering the sick woman's final glimmers of awareness. Then there's a description of the great Parisian doctor who is always brought in at the most desperate moment, dressed in black, wearing his Legion of Honor medal, knowing how to play the role of chief undertaker with great distinction. Finally, the Duc de Guermantes, conscious of the favor he bestows on a bourgeois family by his mere presence, comes to present his condolences in an obsequious and exaggeratedly respectful manner to the hero's mother, who, in the grip of grief, fails to acknowledge the ducal condescension and takes leave of him in the foyer just as he is performing his low bows. It's in the description of such a scene that a great writer's "monstrousness" surfaces; the capacity to analyze, clinically and coolly, to see all the dramatic and humorous details even in life's most tragic moments. I imagine Proust at the bedside of his dying mother, brokenhearted and yet still able to pay attention to all the details, all the tears, all the ridiculous travails of the assembled mourners.

I've spoken about the importance of Proust's psychological analysis of the Faubourg Saint-Germain. Not for nothing did he admire Saint-Simon and Balzac, reading and rereading them, knowing whole pages by heart. In a memoir of the years of Louis XIV, the Duc de Saint-Simon describes in great detail these ancestors of the Faubourg Saint-Germain, their daily lives and gestures, their follies and intrigues. Belonging as he did to the aristocratic elite, Saint-Simon speaks about it firsthand, with great lucidity, as a great writer who can see and record the nuances and absurdities of his own milieu. Balzac's position was quite different. Attracted to the Faubourg Saint-Germain, Balzac was linked, amorously, to women he found there. He had dreams of one day playing the brilliant role of grand seigneur, millionaire, celebrated writer, and heartbreaker all at once. Consumed by work, heavily in debt, filled with fantastic financial plans that regularly ended in disaster, with creditors in hot pursuit, he barely had time to observe this world, barely had the chance to live in it. During the few short moments of respite, when he received a large sum of money from his books or from some other source, he rushed to spend it, childishly buying extravagant costumes which did not always flatter the large paunch he had gotten from being chained to his desk. He bought canes topped in gold and silver; George Sand tells of a reception in Balzac's new lodgings near the Observatoire, where he received her in a salon lit by candelabras, over-decorated with lace curtains, undoubtedly in bad taste as far as the Faubourg Saint-Germain was concerned. In Balzac's consideration of the aristocracy, we meet infinitely lucid and just traits, but I find nowhere in the work of Balzac so much bombast, so much naive idealization, where celestial or in-fernal women recall beings descended from the canvases of romantic painters (for example Prud'hon or even Scheffer) rather than real women in the flesh. Like Balzac, Proust entered this milieu from the outside. But how much more closely he analyzed it, and with how much more personal detachment was he able to judge it! This inside knowledge of the aristocratic life leads me back to Tolstoy, who concerns himself with it in *War and Peace*, *Anna Karenina*, and many other works, with a clarity and a realism less transposed than Proust's. Beginning with Princesse Mathilde, the only his-torical figure of nobility in his book to bear her own name, Proust gathers together his gallery of aristocrats around the

Guermantes and the Baron de Charlus, the brother of the Duc de Guermantes. He ends with parents and friends of the second and third rank orbiting around the sun of the Guermantes family, who represent all the infinite nuances of snobbism, arriviste attitude, and stupidity. Snobbery, more than any other characteristic of this tribe, is studied in all its manifestations. Alongside the high society of Paris, Proust paints us a picture of country aristocracy, simpler, more sympathetic, more attached to real life: the Cambremers, for example. The old baroness is an uncomplicated woman, quite unaffected, a sincere lover of music, proud of having been a student of Chopin in her early youth. Her daughter-in-law, who comes visiting from Paris, is a classic snob about the arts. With neither aptitude nor sentimental or personal artistic talent to link her to art, she strictly adheres to the commonplace notions of the latest fashionable Parisians. Chopin is out. Her humble mother-in-law doesn't dare to say a word about him, almost ashamed to admit how much she loved him, believing that a provincial and backward woman was incapable of discussing him in the definitive, categorical terms of her bluestocking Parisian daughter-in-law. And how touched this old woman is watching the young hero, a true music lover, amuse himself by undermining all of her daughter-in-law's prejudices on his visit to the Cambremers. With what joy, and not without some fear, does she dare to proclaim to the young man her love for Chopin. We sense in these pages that the young hero can distinguish in these women the true from the false in their attitudes toward music. The same holds for painting. He amuses himself by putting the bluestocking in quite awkward situations. The young woman is no doubt aware that he knows infinitely more than she does and that people like him are at the very source of artistic fashion. The bluestocking declares that Poussin is not worth discussing, espousing the currently fashionable naturalist, anticlassical position. The young man replies by saying that Degas (an unimpeachable authority) considers Poussin to be one of the greatest of all French painters. "As soon as I get back to Paris I'll have to go to the Louvre and have another look at his paintings," she replies, completely undone. So, with a light touch, Proust shows us that this woman understands absolutely nothing about art, which she persists in speaking about, that art for her is nothing but a subject for making herself appear more interesting to people even more ignorant than she, and that she believes her position on art gives her the right to look down disdainfully upon people with a genuine interest in art who are not "in the know," as she is.

Proust, speaking about snobbery in all its manifestations, was himself condemned as a perfect snob both in his personal life and even in his work. His earliest school friends wrote him off, convinced that snobbery had derailed him. And even many years later, around 1914 or 1915, at a dinner at the Hôtel Meurice or the Ritz, Misia Godebska-Sert, a brilliant woman who knew everybody from Toulouse-Lautrec and Picasso to the surrealists, asked him whether he wasn't a snob. The next day she was surprised to receive a long letter from him, eight stiff pages (no doubt lost by her), in which he explained how superficial that question was. What wouldn't we give to be able to read that letter today, tossed by her into the trash! Proust's attitude to his life and work was so richly faceted that it seems childish to call him a snob.

From his feelings for the Duchesse de Guermantes seen against the medieval stained glass windows of the Combray church, on through to his love for that same duchess and his fascination with the world of society he discovers, right up to his severest remarks, to his observations and his awareness of all their faults—their pettiness, coldness, impotence, and stupidity—we find all of this in his books. With what degree of acuity Proust is able to know, to intuit, the character of the young Guermantes nephew, a soldier crazy for music and literature, noble in character and in all his impulses, who dies heroically during a bombing in the war! With what humor, at the same time, he shows us the inbred stupidity of all sorts of worldly aristocrats, and adds in one of his books this disenchanted sentence: "He'd be charming if he weren't so stupid." Furthermore, Proust's attitude as a writer toward this milieu is as completely detached, I would say scientifically objective, as it is toward Françoise the cook, the clan of doctors, or even toward his own grandmother. He compares the kitchen where Françoise reigns in Combray with the court of Louis XIV, the Sun King, and all the intrigues surrounding it. When speaking of aristocrats, he discovers conflicting affinities. He describes an encounter between the hero, in the courtyard of his house, and his landlord, the Duc de Guermantes, who cannot resist picking off several stray hairs from the velvet collar of the young man's coat with a light touch of his hand, with an extreme gentleness and obsequious politeness during their conversation. "It's not only the lackeys of very great houses and representatives of the finest aristocratic families," Proust notes, "who possess this reflex." He goes on to develop a whole theory of nuanced relationships based on the provenance of aristocrats and the role they had to play at Versailles.

A key theme of *À la recherche* must be raised once again. It's the question of physical love, which Proust studies in all its veiled and secret aspects. All its anomalies and perversions are considered by Proust with the same analytic detachment, neither whitewashed nor blackened. Balzac, Proust's great precursor, had the courage to treat this subject earlier, in *Vautrin* and *La Fille aux yeux d'or*, in a manner more circumspect than most. After twenty years of postwar literature that deals with everything in the domain of sexuality in a cynical and exhibitionist manner (Proust is quite reserved if we think of certain chapters of Céline), we have become accustomed to it, and so often fatigued and annoyed by it, that it's barely comprehensible to us that certain pages of *Du côté de chez Swann*—touching on the lesbian amours of Vinteuil's daughter—published just before 1914, or the story of the grand seigneur Charlus, whose position in society collapses due to a scandal à la Oscar Wilde and whom we see yielding to the worst masochistic deviations in a Paris dive—that these pages, conceived and written before the war of 1914, represented an act of courage. Proust shone a penetrating light into the most secret recesses of the human soul that the majority of humanity would prefer to ignore. In this domain, as in all his other studies—of the aristocracy, of filial love, of secrets hidden in the mechanics of artistic creation, etc.—we encounter the same Proust, with his admirable lucidity and an analytic apparatus of a precision and meticulousness unknown before him.

5

I'D LIKE to stress some conclusions I've come to, which might suggest still others. With his revelatory form, Proust brings a world of ideas to the reader, a complete vision of life that, by awakening his faculties of thought and feeling, requires the reader to revise his own scale of values. I'd like to make clear, as I've already said before, that we are not subjected to any narrow-mindedness in his work. Nothing is more foreign to Proust than a tendentious work. Often he repeats this himself, saying that only by pushing a form to its furthest limits can one possibly manage to begin to convey the essence of a writer.

In the final volume of the novel, *Le Temps retrouvé*, Proust offhandedly engages in polemics with Barrès. The leader of a group of young nationalist writers at the time, Barrès was himself a great writer. Throughout his books *Les Déracinés* and *La Colline inspirée*, he stressed the nationalist side of a writer's work. Originally from Lorraine, Barrès felt that the deepest source of inspiration could come only from the earth, from the soil, from pure French traditions. (It's against this idea of Barrès that Gide wrote his critical study on uprootedness, in which he, to the contrary, emphasized the positive effects of making contact with a wider world.) Barrès declared that a writer must never forget that he is a nationalist writer, and must delve into this element in his work. Proust, in passing, responds to him in a sentence that, unfortunately, I can only repeat inexactly, summarily, and my paraphrase risks trivializing it: Barrès states that a writer, before becoming a writer, must acknowledge his role and his mission as a Frenchman.

A scientist, on the verge of a discovery, can succeed only by giving his search the full attention of *all* his faculties, he is in no condition to think of anything else. In the same way, for the writer, it is not this or that idea he expounds by which we ought to measure the contribution that he has given to his country, but rather by the limits he pushes against in the realization of his form. Even among the greatest writers, single-mindedness weakens the effect of a work and can be a disservice, not only from an artistic point of view, but also in consideration of the very ideas that the writer had wanted to serve. If we look at our own literary landscape, we'll find examples that are both surprising and tragically instructive. There are the examples of Żeromski and Conrad-Korzeniowski. We never find the slightest veering towards didacticism in their work, never a tendentious note. Nevertheless, admittedly, Conrad's work awakens in the attentive reader a world of ideas and problems. Son of an exiled Polish revolutionary, Conrad was born on Russian soil. He was a man who worshipped the basic sentiments of loyalty and honor throughout his life, who had to leave his country, leave his language, and become a writer in a foreign language in a foreign land, all in order to find an atmosphere where he might be capable of producing a body of work free of immediate bias, a work free of didacticism. Żeromski, the man who did the most to champion him in Poland, made Conrad a Polish writer once again.

But Żeromski also had to do battle with him, as did

Orzeszkowa, who banished Conrad to the realm of traitors for having left Poland at the very moment her sons were needed. Żeromski strikes me as no less talented a writer than Conrad, albeit terribly uneven. He didn't leave his country, which he loved more than anything, even more than art. He wrote his books with the idea that they could always be useful to his country, and one can truly apply to him words that Krasiński uttered after the death of Mickiewicz: "He was the blood, the milk, and the honey of our generation." But Żeromski was too great an artist not to understand that he often sacrificed perfection in his work for a more noble cause, albeit a utilitarian one. And in his own assessment, which has already appeared among free Poles, he says with a touching humility, "I had such a desire to reawaken consciousness in my compatriots, to push them toward generosity and heroism, that through this tendency I abandoned artistic values and, even without that, weakened my own work." And yet it was Żeromski who advocated on Conrad's behalf, writing an introduction to the first volume of Conrad to be translated into Polish, *The Nigger of the "Narcissus."* He saw Conrad not as a traitor but as a brother who in a freer world was able to realize what Żeromski had had to sacrifice, and what in a free Poland seemed to him the most indispensable nourishment for the younger generation.

Leaving aside the realm of Polish letters, we can discover this harmful effect of tendentiousness in a writer who was perhaps the great novelist of his time. In *War and Peace* and in *Anna Karenina*, one finds hardly a trace of didacticism. Revising *Anna Karenina*, Tolstoy rewrote a long passage in order to hide his own opinion from the reader. But in *Resurrection*, the grand novel of his old age, we meet didacticism all too clearly, the author voicing certain key ideas so often that it produced the opposite effect, putting readers off, and so even Tolstoy, by lowering the artistic standard of his work, weakens rather than strengthens the radiance of his ideas.

Proust is the complete opposite. In his work we come across an absolute absence of bias, a willingness to know and to understand as many opposing states of the human soul as possible, a capacity for discovering in the lowest sort of man such nobility as to appear sublime, and in the seemingly purest of beings, the basest instincts. His work acts on us like life, filtered and illuminated by a consciousness whose soundness is infinitely greater than our own.

Readers of Proust might be surprised to hear me say that the ideological conclusions of *À la recherche* that touch me most personally are almost Pascalian. I recall being greatly surprised when reading an article by Boy on Proust where he spoke of that "delicious" Charlus. It was clear to me from the tone of the piece that what Boy found to be essential in Proust was the work's humor and *joie de vivre*. I've barely spoken with you about Pascal, but we all know about his completely anti-sensual sensibility. This man, devoured by a yearning for the absolute, considered all the ephemeral joys of the senses unacceptable. A physicist of genius, celebrated in the most refined company in France, he was full of pride and an innate, ambitious hunger. This man passed a night that will always remain known as Pascal's mystery, a night yielding an intense vision of a super-terrestrial world which caused him forever after, until his death, to wear around his neck a small scrap of paper on which was inscribed these few words: "Tears, tears of joy." Pascal broke with everything and with everyone, threw himself with his entire passionate nature into an extreme asceticism and holed up in Port-Royal, exhausting himself, torturing his poor body to the point of great suffering. Not only did he swallow the food he ate in such a way that he couldn't taste it, not only did he wear an iron belt, but he even guarded himself against his most elevated passions—mathematics, physics, literature itself—all the while jotting down, but only episodically, ideas which, gathered together after his death, amount to one of the most concise, profound, and ardent books in all of world literature. Pascal ridiculed not only the offending senses he rejected, but all the senses. The terrible phrase, "Marriage, the lowest condition of Christianity," belongs to Pascal. It may then seem paradoxical that I link Pascalian thoughts with *À la recherche*, a book that seems entirely devoted to the study of the senses, that contains thousands of pages written by a man who relished the sensory joys of the earth, who knew how to enjoy everything to the furthest extent possible in a way that was passionate, refined, and fully aware. I know about a short, unpublished letter Proust wrote to his friend from lycée, Daniel Halévy, probably in response to some moralistic remarks or advice Halévy offered, Proust declared that there was only one thing he desired: to take pleasure in a life of joy and physical love. We mustn't forget that the world around Anatole France was his first literary milieu, and the strongly hedonistic religion of this great French writer undoubtedly exerted its influence on the formation of Proust's world of ideas. It has often been said that Proust's whole body of work lacks any religious inquiry, that the word "God" never appears, not once, in its thousands of pages. And yet, or maybe even especially because of this, such an apotheosis of all of life's fleeting pleasures leaves us with a taste of Pascalian ash in our mouths. It's not in the name of God, nor in the name of religion, that the protagonist of *À la recherche* rejects everything, yet he, too, like Pascal, is struck by a shattering revelation: he also buries himself, half-alive, in his cork-lined room (here I willingly blur the distinction between the hero and Proust himself since in this case they are one) to serve until death what became for him an absolute, his artistic work. The last volume of his novel, *Le Temps retrouvé*, likewise mixed with "tears of joy," is the triumphant hymn of a man who has sold all his worldly possessions to buy a single precious pearl, who has measured all the ephemera, all the heartbreak, all the vanity of the joys of the world, of youth, of fame, of eroticism, and holds them up in comparison with the joy of the artist, this being who, in constructing each sentence, making and then remaking each page, is in search of an absolute he can never entirely attain, and which, besides, is ultimately unattainable.

VANITY

The vanity of worldly relations. Swann, the perfect man of the world, seriously ill, receives a sentence of death from his doctors: he won't live more than another two or three months. In the courtyard of the Hôtel de Guermantes, just as the Duc and the Duchesse are hurriedly taking off for a big party, Swann decides to announce this news to the Duchesse, his best friend, the reigning queen of Paris. The couple has to choose between hearing about the death sentence and risk being late for a grand dinner. To avoid this, they make a mockery of his news, reassuring poor Swann, with his cadaverous face, that he certainly looks marvelous; they leave him standing alone there in the surround of their magnificent townhouse. A moment later the duke notices that the duchess's shoes are not the color he expected to see on her: they don't match her red velvet dress and her ruby necklace. While Swann has not succeeded in detaining them for even a few moments, shoes of the wrong color do. Their departure is delayed by a quarter of an hour.

The vanity of aristocratic pride. In *Le Temps retrouvé*, Proust depicts a sumptuous reception at the same Hôtel de Guermantes. But the princess of this family of the purest blood, celebrated for her rare finesse and unique style, has, after her death, been replaced by Duchesse de Guermantes number two, a wealthy bourgeoise, pickled in snobbery, vulgarity, and the ridiculous. The postwar party guests, among them rich American women from overseas, accept and admire her without suspecting at all that she and the once renowned Princesse de Guermantes are unrelated except in title and position.

Vanity of youth and beauty. "The irreparable ravages of time"*—Odette, the beguiling courtesan, the passion of Swann and many others, the wife of Swann, then of the Comte de Forcheville, incarnating throughout Proust's work everything seductive in a woman, is represented by him in the final volume as a nearly idiotic old woman huddled in her daughter's salon. Having once been surrounded by luxuries and attention, she is now barely noticed. Upon entering, each guest approaches her and makes a deep bow but, once two steps away, feels free to forget her or even, in a loud voice, to speak of her with mockery or wickedness. And Proust, who, as I've said before, maintains a cruel objectivity everywhere, adds here a comment that is unexpected because it's tenderly personal: "And this woman, adulated and worshipped

*Racine, *Athalie*, II, 5.

her whole life, now a human wreck in formal dress and *grande toilette*, looks out alarmed and bewildered at the ferocious social world and seems to me for the first time . . . likable."

Vanity, the futility of fame. The great actress Berma, a barely transposed Sarah Bernhardt, provides Proust the opportunity to write some inimitable pages. The actress is old and sick: she can no longer play her scenes except when drugged, after which she spends her nights in pain and insomnia at her home on one of the Parisian riverbanks. Only towards morning are a few hours of sleep possible. But her beloved daughter, for whom alone she endures all these tortures, wants to build an identical townhouse immediately adjacent to her mother's. From the crack of dawn, the uninterrupted noise of hammering makes sleep impossible for Berma. Around this time, a third-rate actress, much younger than Berma, decides to take revenge on her. By means of intrigue, connections, and baseness she gains the favor of a less discriminating postwar public. She chooses the aging Berma's "at home" day to make her own debut in the fashionable world. She plans to read quasi-modern poetry at a party where *le tout Paris* will gather. As a result, the old and gifted actress finds her own salon completely empty that evening, except for a quite young man, not yet in the know, and her daughter and son-in-law, furious about having to spend the evening with their ancient mother and not in the brilliant and crowded salon of the Princesse de Guermantes. Proust describes the delicate bone structure of Berma's face, dusted with powder, her eyes still animated "like the serpents of the Erechtheion marbles." Her adored daughter strikes the final blow. Abandoning her mother's salon, she hurries, with her husband, uninvited, to the grand reception, to have the honor of being present at the triumph of her mother's worst enemy. Like a hunted beast, the daughter manages to be introduced into these rooms through the intervention of this actress, who is only too pleased to lash out and wound Berma by disdainfully patronizing her daughter.

The vanity of love. The caprices, the passions, the entanglements of love; what do these hold for those completely dedicated to them? We see Baron de Charlus, aging, cast aside by society, in a brothel, engaging in monstrous masochistic practices, chained to his desires like Prometheus to his rock. Then we see the same Charlus, reduced to a second childhood, in a wheelchair, blind and incapable of walking on his own, being led about by the tailor Jupien, a shady friend from his early days and the proprietor of the brothel, who is the only one looking after the old man, seeing to his needs with an almost maternal affection.

In *À la recherche*, the hero's greatest love is for Albertine. *À l'ombre des jeunes filles en fleurs* is filled with description of the exquisite charms of the quite young Albertine and her sporty friends. In *Sodom et Gomorrhe*, in *Albertine*, we enter into the world of love, of jealousy, of tenderness aroused by the young girl. *Albertine disparue* is simply a cry of distress, a relentless pursuit made after the fleeing young girl, a jealous and painful investigation of her entire past. When, after barely a year, the hero learns, during a visit to Venice, of the sudden death of this woman he loved, he pays the news scant attention because he's momentarily preoccupied with someone else. And with what supreme detachment moreover (which has nothing in common with the anti-carnal rage of a Pascal) does the very author, who has himself suffered so much, speak about love toward the end of his numerous volumes. He speaks of it from a rather utilitarian point of view, counseling a love slightly mired in the flesh as the best antidote for the disenchantment of worldly joys, proposing it in place of a fondness for the social whirl which can bring the greatest disarray into an artist's life. Proust makes one point over and over: the artist is and must be solitary. Students, even disciples, weaken the artist, and while his views on love are entirely pessimistic, seeing love only as the cause of "costly injury and increased awareness of loneliness," there is one enjoyment he is hesitantly willing to allow in the realm of the senses. At the moment he decides to bury himself in his work, to take leave of the world and its ephemeral joys, he announces that maybe, even so, he will permit himself amorous flings with charming young girls from time to time—he refuses to be like that horse of antiquity who was fed only roses.

DEATH—THE APPROACH OF DEATH

If we want to guess at Proust's final thoughts about life and death, those born at the moment as, after years of experience, he approached his own end, it's the character Bergotte, a character of secondary importance, who might provide the key. In *À la recherche*, Bergotte is a great writer, a master of the French language, who embodies, for the very young hero, all the beauties of literature. The materials that served Proust in the creation of this character stem from his observation and study of Anatole France, many of whose traits Bergotte shares, and from Proust's own intimate experience of himself, the Proust of his final period.

We first encounter the name Bergotte in *Du côté de chez Swann*. The young hero discovers his books, declares Bergotte his preferred master, and dreams of meeting him. It's in *Le Côté de Guermantes*, I believe, that he meets him for the first time, in the salon of Odette, already Madame Swann.* He meets him there, an old friend of Swann's who speaks to him in an extremely considerate fashion, and offers him a lift home in his carriage at the end of the visit. From the first moment, moreover, this acquaintance gives rise to a common disappointment. In flesh and blood, Bergotte bears little resemblance to the writer the young man had dreamed of meeting. What so surprises him is that during their ride home, Bergotte, a dear friend of Swann, begins to speak ill of his friend with great discernment, detachment, and ease, to a young boy he has only just met for the first time. Bergotte provides Proust, with his lucid and just mind, the opportunity to study all the weaknesses, all the small and large acts of cowardice, all the lies so often encountered in artists. In the following volumes we watch Bergotte age at the time of his greatest renown, his creative powers in decline. He writes books less and less frequently—works of an inferior quality, the writing requiring more effort, relying on feelings of internal necessity and joy that are considerably weakened—and he likes to repeat the following sentence: "I think that in writing my books, I have been useful to my country," a sentence he would never have uttered at the time he was writing his greatest works. In all these psychological remarks and descriptions, we sense not Proust himself providing material for the character, but mostly Anatole France (and also perhaps Barrès).

But in the pages devoted to Bergotte's final illness and death in *Albertine* and *Albertine disparue* we come closer to

* This scene occurs in *À l'ombre des jeunes filles en fleurs*.

the state of Proust's own soul and body. These passages appear in the final volume corrected by Proust before his death, and we know that his corrections to the proofs were often quite extensive. He would add, rewrite, or cross out tens and even hundreds of pages—the same vice that literally undermined Balzac. Proust recounts in detail all the bound-together hopes and deceptions in the relationship between a sick person and his doctor. He catalogues all the kinds of sleep, all the drugs and sleeping drafts that Bergotte, exhausted by insomnia, was addicted to at the time of his death. Certain features describing Bergotte's final stage of illness were inserted by Proust barely days before his own death.

At an exhibition of the work of the great Dutch painter Vermeer, the favorite painter of Swann and Bergotte, the latter is struck down. By chance I learned that once the war was over, several years before the death of Proust, his friend, the critic Jean-Louis Vaudoyer, took him to see a show of Dutch painting. While there, Proust was struck by a serious cardiac attack. In *Albertine*, Bergotte decides to go have a look at the canvases of Vermeer one more time before he dies, though he knows well enough that, given his health, it's risky for him to go out to see the exhibition. Immediately upon arrival, he is completely taken in by the mysterious charm, the Chinese perfection and delicacy, the tender music of these canvases. He stops, full of admiration, before a landscape of some houses on the beach at the seaside. He notices some very small blue figures on the yellow sand, a little patch of yellow wall, gilded by the rays of the sun. Here he makes a final assessment of his consciousness as a writer. "Little patch of yellow wall, little patch of yellow wall," he repeats in a low voice, "that's how I ought to have written my books, going back over and over the same sentences, reworking them, enriching them, superimposing layers on them like this patch of wall. My sentences were too dry and too little worked over." And here, at this moment, a sentence issues forth in a low voice from Bergotte-Proust, all the more surprising coming from a student of Anatole France: "What does this relentless work by a virtually unknown artist mean, in its observation of barely visible details; what could justify such an unremitting effort towards an end that probably no one will notice, or comprehend, or most likely even see? It's as if we live under laws of justice, of absolute truth, of perfect effort, which were created in another world of harmony and truth, whose reflections appear to us on earth and guide us." This short passage might be overlooked or neglected by an inattentive reader, a reader who has not realized the extreme sense of responsibility Proust brought to each of his sentences. But we know that these pages were revised by the author just before his death, that they became like a sacred grove amidst the thousands of pages written by a student of *La Revolte des anges*.* And suddenly by association another great writer comes to mind; a writer who, from start to finish in his work, was possessed by a single problem, the problem of God and immortality: "Many things in life are hidden from us," writes Dostoevsky in *The Brothers Karamazov,* spoken by Zosima. "But in exchange, we are given the intimate feeling of a link with another world, a higher world. Even the roots of our thoughts and feelings are not here, but in other worlds."

Dostoevsky goes on to say that everything lives in us thanks to this intimate feeling of connection; that should

*Anatole France's ironic 1914 novella about nationalism and the tyranny of the Church.

the connection be broken, we would become indifferent to life, we might even come to hate it. At the very moment Bergotte begins to understand what art must be—looking back on the strengths and weaknesses of his life's work in light of the little patch of yellow wall painted by the master of Delft—he senses a heart attack coming on. He tries to sit down on a bench, reassuring himself that it's nothing, probably just a symptom of indigestion: he had needlessly eaten some potatoes. But this lasts only a few seconds. His condition worsens precipitously and without reaching the bench Bergotte falls to the ground, struck down, dead.

Proust produces one more sentence about him: "Bergotte is dead; dead for good?" He expands on this sentence, which reminds us of Dostoevsky, by suggesting it's not impossible Bergotte might not be utterly broken and destroyed. And Proust ends with a sublimely poetic sentence which I'm incapable of repeating to you word for word: "And all night, in all the illuminated windows of the bookshops of Paris, his books, open three by three, kept vigil like angels with their wings unfurled over the body of the dead writer."

The death of Bergotte and the long illness that precedes it are forever tied in my memory to the death of Proust. I would like to conclude these reminiscences with such details as I can recall. In his last years Proust's health worsened more and more. His friends were unaware of the gravity of the situation because, on the rare occasions they had a chance to see him, he was brilliant, full of verve and soulfulness. As his work began to appear, volume after volume, his readers were dazzled. There's a description of Proust in these late years in the memoir of Léon-Paul Fargue: dressed to the hilt with his greenish complexion and his black, almost blue, hair, standing against a background of Bonnard's violet and silver canvases at a party at the home of Misia Godebska-Sert. Fargue notes that this Proust was quite different from the worldly, nervous young man from before the war, that he had something uncannily mature in his smile and comportment. One sensed in him a distance, a detachment, a certitude. Also dating from these last years is a letter from Proust that Mauriac refers to in his *Journal*: "I want to see you. For whole weeks I was not to be seen, I kept to my shroud, I was dead." Proust underlined the word "dead" in his letter. Since Proust had always been sick, it was easy to dismiss this as literary exaggeration, far from the truth. But the doctors saw clearly that his condition was deteriorating day by day, dragged down by "a terrible neglect of health, brought on by his work," by his having lost faith in any remedy, in any regime they might have wanted to impose on him. He fell into atrocious fits of anger when his doctor-brother wanted to force him to take care of himself. It's not possible that he did not understand, given the state of his health, that the enormous and feverish effort required to keep on with his work would precipitate his end. But he had made up his mind, he would not take care of himself; death had become truly a matter of indifference to him.

Death came and took him as he deserved to be taken, hard at work. They found him dead in the morning in his bed. On his nightstand a flask of medicine had been overturned, its liquid blackening a little sheet of paper on which had been written that same night, in his fine, nervous handwriting, the name of a not-even-secondary character from *À la recherche*: Forcheville.

GLOSSARY OF SELECTED NAMES

LÉONTINE ARMAN DE CAILLAVET (1844–1910)
French society hostess
From a family of German Jewish bankers, fluent in four languages, and married to Albert Arman de Caillavet (who wrote a yachting column for *Le Figaro*), Léontine Lippmann established a formidable literary, political, and artistic salon in her *hôtel particulier* near Place de l'Étoile. This gathering was frequented by Marcel Proust from the time he was nineteen. Madame Arman's slightly overbearing tendency to guide the conversations of dinner guests would resurface in the novelist's unflattering portrait of Madame Verdurin. Her son, Gaston, Proust's friend from his year of military service, figured in the lineage of the novel's most dashing character, Robert de Saint-Loup. Madame Arman exerted considerable nurturing influence on the literary career of her lover, the novelist Anatole France.

MAURICE BARRÈS (1862–1923)
French novelist and political activist
Barrès forged his reputation as a novelist with his youthful trilogy *Le Culte de moi* (*The Cult of the Self,* 1888–1891), a paean to individualism and sensualism. The eruption of the Dreyfus Affair in 1894 triggered a change in him. Incensed by any challenge to the authority of the army, he lashed out,

making frequent use of the term "nationalism" to inflame anti-Semitic discourse. A second trilogy, *Le Roman de l'énergie nationale* (*The Novel of National Energy*, 1897–1902), espoused a proto-fascist subjugation of the individual to nation and tradition. The two trilogies made him one of the most popular, influential, and controversial writers of his generation. Proust refers to Barrès by name in the last volume of his novel, identifying him with the sin of tendentiousness, a willingness to make a single point over and over again at the expense of the artistic integrity of a book.

HENRI BERGSON (1859–1941)
French philosopher and essayist
The most prominent philosopher of his generation and the recipient of the 1927 Nobel Prize in Literature, Bergson exerted an influence on Proust that was profound and substantial. Born into a family of Polish Jews, he was a student at the Lycée Condorcet a few years ahead of Proust and became a dynamic teacher whose scientific and philosophic lectures would inspire the novelist's own shrewd examination of memory. Bergson gave his inaugural lecture at the Collège de France in 1900, with Proust in attendance; it was an event that would have a significant impact on European thought and culture. On the subject of Proust's relationship to Bergson, Czapski says, "as far as I recall, he knew the man personally." Proust not only knew Bergson, they were related by marriage, Bergson having married Proust's second cousin Louise Neuberger in 1891. Marcel, then twenty, was best man at their wedding.

LÉON BLOY (1846–1917)
French novelist and poet

After an unhappy childhood in the Dordogne, Bloy was sent to work at a job in Paris found for him by his father. Under the sympathetic tutelage of his neighbor, the Byronic novelist Barbey d'Aurevilly, Bloy forswore the agnosticism of his youth and became a devout Catholic. His novel *La Femme pauvre*, the story of a poor woman who becomes an artist's model, is full of compassion and Catholic allusions. A visionary and a polemicist, he set out to convert many of his intellectual colleagues to his faith. The theologian Jacques Maritain called him "a Christian of the second century astray in the Third Republic." Impoverished throughout his life, his tenets were controversial; he saw modern life and thought as tending inevitably to catastrophe. His books resurfaced in print some years after his death, just as Czapski arrived in Paris.

MATHILDE BONAPARTE (Princesse Mathilde; 1820–1904)
French aristocrat and hostess

The only member of the Bonaparte family to remain in France after the emergence of the Third Republic, Princess Mathilde was the daughter of Napoleon's brother. She understood perfectly well the circumstantial nature of her elevation in society. Never imperious, she told Proust that if her uncle had not been Napoleon she would "most likely be selling oranges on the streets of Ajaccio." Untransfigured, she makes an appearance in the second volume of Proust's novel, where she tells the guests at a party that whenever she was inclined to pay a visit to her uncle's tomb at Les Invalides, she would let herself in with her own key.

CHARLES BOSON DE TALLEYRAND-PÉRIGORD (Prince
    Sagan; 1832–1910)
French aristocrat
Among the elite of French society, the prince lived a life of
luxury in a world not yet aware of its imminent demise. His
dandyish appearance reflected a personal style and grace and
he was susceptible to the many temptations with which he
found himself surrounded. Proust studied him carefully and
used these observations in his description of the elegant Duc
de Guermantes, whose given name, Basin, is very close to the
prince's name, Boson. Prince Sagan's comportment and his
arrogance also surface in Proust's Falstaffian Baron de Charlus. Like Charlus, the aging Boson de Talleyrand-Périgord
suffered a debilitating stroke and was reduced to a state of
dependency, pushed about in a wheelchair by a servant.

JACQUES BOULENGER (1879–1944)
French literary critic
In his essay *Contre Sainte-Beuve*, Proust singled out Boulenger
for praise, and Boulenger, a specialist in medieval literature,
defended Proust from the many critics who attacked him
after he won the Goncourt Prize in 1919. Near the end of his
life, however, Proust wrote a contentious letter to *La Nouvelle
Revue Française* about an article Boulenger had written on
the subject of Flaubert, only to retract it before publication.
Before and during World War II, Boulenger wrote for an
increasingly right-wing journal and edited a series of anti-
Semitic pamphlets.

TADEUSZ BOY-ŻELEŃSKI (1874–1941)
Polish doctor, writer, and translator
After serving as a medic in World War I, Boy, as he was

generally called, settled in Warsaw, abandoning the practice of medicine to devote himself to the theater and to writing. In addition to his own essays on a wide range of intellectual and political subjects, he translated over one hundred French texts into Polish, not least of which were several volumes of Proust's *À la recherche du temps perdu*. Czapski, on being released from Gryazovets, first heard a rumor that Boy-Żeleński had died of illness in a concentration camp, but he later learned that his friend had been murdered by the Nazis, along with more than 160 other professors from the University of Lwów. Boy's translation of *À la recherche* was unfinished at the time of his death. In Poland he is celebrated for his sensitivity to the music in words and his translations continue to be considered masterpieces of the Polish language.

BLAISE CENDRARS (pen name of Frédéric-Louis Sauser; 1887–1961)
Swiss-born French poet, novelist, and journalist
Following in the footsteps of Rimbaud, Cendrars rejected the trappings of a "man of letters" and wrote from an impulse that was neither literary or aesthetic. He fought with the French Foreign Legion during the Battle of the Somme and lost his right arm in battle. One of the first modernist poets in France, he was a devoted friend to many painters whose work was powerfully influenced by the new art of cinema. Modigliani painted his portrait. In the 1930s Cendrars went to the United States on assignment for the magazine *Paris-Soir*, and later wrote a book about Hollywood.

DUCHESSE DE CLERMONT-TONNERRE (1875–1954)
French writer
Of impeccable pedigree, Proust's friend Élisabeth de Gramont, known as "Lily," was an impressive woman, physically beautiful in her youth and highly intelligent. A descendant of Henry IV, she married the Duc de Clermont-Tonnere, bore two daughters, and then fell in love with the American writer Natalie Barney in 1909. The two women became lovers and maintained a conjugal bond for the remainder of Élisabeth's life. She was nicknamed "The Red Duchess" in honor of her sympathy for the socialist cause. The Duchesse de Clermont-Tonnere wrote a family history that was widely praised, as well as an admiring book about her friend Proust.

ERNST ROBERT CURTIUS (1886–1956)
German literary scholar, philologist, and critic
Between the years 1922 and 1924, before the final volumes of *À la recherche du temps perdu* were published, Curtius wrote a thoughtful book-length appreciation of Proust, whose compelling use of the French language appealed to his German formalist sensibility. "One perceives an unknown music," Curtius wrote, "whose harmonies one has no means to analyze." Throughout the Second World War, a time when French culture was considered suspect and inferior in Germany, Curtius continued to champion the importance of French literature.

SERGEI DIAGHILEV (1872–1929)
Russian impresario
Diaghilev first made his mark in Paris curating an exhibition of Russian paintings at the Petit Palais in 1906. Returning to France in the following years, he expanded his reputation

with the Ballets Russes, a company he founded to bring together some of Russia's finest dancers, musicians, and painters. The troupe made an indelible impression on European culture. Once established as a sensation in Paris, Diaghilev drew many French artists into the fold, providing a cross-fertilization of talent rarely seen before or since. The impact of these performances on Proust cannot be overestimated. Impulsive, shrewd, and perceptive, Diaghilev established himself as Europe's supreme entrepreneur of the arts. Czapski was directly connected to the Diaghilev circle through his friendship with the Russian philosopher Dmitri Filosofov.

LÉON-PAUL FARGUE (1876–1947)
French poet and essayist
A student of Mallarmé and Bergson, Fargue is best known for his atmospheric evocations of Paris, where he was born, lived, and died. He was a great walker of the city's streets. His writings were primarily symbolist in form and content, invoking the oppressive solitude of the night and the effect of alcohol on perception. In his memoirs, Fargue writes about his encounters with Proust. Their mutual friend, Misia Godebska-Sert, suggested Fargue write the introduction for a catalogue of Czapski's first exhibition of paintings shown in Paris.

CLAUDE FARRÈRE (pen name of Frédéric-Charles
    Bargone; 1876–1957)
French novelist
A member of the Académie française and winner of the Prix Goncourt, Farrère was a prolific writer whose stories were generally set in exotic locations. Having been a naval officer who sailed around the world, he drew on his travels

for inspiration and wrote a history of the French Navy. He published four novels in 1925 alone.

RAMON FERNANDEZ (1894–1944)
French literary critic

Fernandez was the author of over a dozen monographs on European writers. His grandfather had been mayor of Mexico City, but he was born in Paris where his father was posted as an attaché to the Mexican embassy. His mother was a French fashion writer, one of the founders of French *Vogue*. Fernandez was sought out and befriended by Proust, who wrote to him to say that it was not his beautiful face but his beautiful mind "that I desire to know in you." Late one night during the First World War, as a German bombing raid exploded over Paris, Proust appeared at Fernandez's door and politely asked his young protégé to pronounce two words for him in Italian—*senza rigore*, a musical term indicating a relaxation of strict rules, of strict tempi. Czapski attributes to Fernandez the idea that these words surface in a scene where Albertine is having a conversation about driving a car, but his recall is mistaken. The words are uttered not by Albertine, as Czapski suggests, but rather by Odette, in another scene, when she remarks that her salon is much more casual than that of her rival, Madame Verdurin. In the two sets of typescript made from Czapski's dictation, the Italian words appear as *senza vigore*; apparently both recording scribes must have misunderstood him, because *senza rigore* appears correctly written out in Czapski's hand in one of his schematic diagrams.

One of only a few people Proust received in the last year of his life, Fernandez would become the founding editor of *Cahiers Marcel Proust*, the first journal dedicated to all things Proustian.

MARIA GODEBSKA-SERT (1872–1950)
Parisian society hostess and pianist
Godebska's father was a prominent Polish sculptor; her Russian-Belgian cellist mother died giving birth to her. Raised by her grandparents in a musical world which included Franz Liszt, she was a student of Fauré. Known to one and all as Misia, she married Thadée Natanson, the nephew of her stepmother's first husband. Together the young couple flourished on the Parisian social scene, hosting a salon that attracted many of the major figures in the arts of the time, including Monet, Debussy, and Mallarmé. Toulouse-Lautrec often played the role of bartender at their gatherings. Coco Chanel and Diaghilev were her great friends. The Natansons launched *La Revue blanche*, a lavishly illustrated literary journal in which Proust published some of his first small pieces. In 1914, following the collapse of her second marriage, Misia married the Spanish painter José-Maria Sert. She entertained a mixture of bohemian and high-society friends in great style and provided invaluable support to Czapski at the beginning of his career as a painter.

CHARLES HAAS (1833–1902)
French society figure
In a group portrait painted by James Tissot, *Le Cercle de la rue Royale*, Charles Haas appears on the far right of the wide canvas, standing on the threshold of the club's balcony, simultaneously part of the gathering and separate from it. The only Jewish member of the Jockey Club, and a close friend of the Prince of Wales, Haas adeptly navigated the exacting protocols of French society. According to his friend Boniface de Castellane, Haas "belonged to that category of witty and useless idlers who were like an extravagance of the society of the time and whose principal merit consisted of gossiping,

before dinner, at the 'Jockey' or the Duchesse de Trémoille's." For many years, he and Sarah Bernhardt were lovers. Haas befriended and supported many painters. Proust breaks through the literary fourth wall in the pages of *La Prison-nière* to address Haas directly, acknowledging the man-about-town's part in the formation of the character Charles Swann.

DANIEL HALÉVY (1872–1962)
French historian

Great-nephew of the composer of the opera *La Juive*, Daniel Halévy was born into a talented and thoroughly assimilated Parisian-Jewish family. A schoolmate and friend of Proust at the Lycée Condorcet, he was also for a time the object of the budding novelist's inflamed desire. Edgar Degas, a close family friend, was a formidable presence in his childhood and adolescence. In the 1920s, soon after Proust died, Czapski appeared on Halévy's doorstep in Paris and the two men became very close friends, despite a difference in age of two decades. Halévy wrote an introduction to the French edition of Czapski's memoir of his wartime experiences in Soviet Russia, *Inhuman Land*. Active as a young man in the defense of Alfred Dreyfus, Halévy became politically more conservative as he aged. He hated fascism, but endorsed Marshal Pétain and the Vichy regime.

ZYGMUNT KRASIŃSKI (1812–1859)
Polish poet and playwright

Descended from a long line of aristocratic Polish families, Krasiński was born in Paris and lived most of his life in France and Italy. He is one of a trio of major poets of Polish romanticism, alongside Juliusz Słowacki and Adam Mickiewicz, all three of whom came to creative maturity while Poland was under foreign subjugation, as it remained throughout the nineteenth century. Krasiński was the most conservative of the three poets, embracing the notion of a ruling elite, distancing himself from any talk of revolution, even when national independence was at stake. Krasiński's metaphysical drama, *The Undivine Comedy*, expresses his belief that any story of man in a historical context is inherently a tragedy.

HENRI-RENÉ LENORMAND (1882–1951)
French dramatist
Lenormand made a career writing plays for the Paris stage, largely symbolist in nature, with a special interest in the subconscious motivations of his characters. Laid up in bed in Switzerland while undergoing treatment for tuberculosis, he read Strindberg and Freud, little known in France at the time. Their works would influence his development as a playwright and a drama critic.

PIERRE LOTI (pen name of Julien Viaud; 1850–1923)
French novelist
A member of the Académie française, Loti was a prolific writer whose stories were generally set in India, Asia, and the South Pacific. His work was the inspiration for the 1883 opera *Lakmé* by Léo Delibes, and he collaborated with Reynaldo Hahn, Proust's great love, on another opera. Loti was a favorite writer of the adolescent Proust, who gave his mother a copy of Loti's *Le Roman d'un enfant* when her mother, his beloved grandmother, died.

FRANÇOIS MAURIAC (1885–1970)
French writer
Recipient of the 1952 Nobel Prize in Literature, Mauriac was a young friend of the ailing Proust. As much as he is known for his novels, poetry, and plays, he is remembered today as

a public figure of moral integrity, having taken a stand against French rule in Vietnam and the use of torture in Algeria. A Catholic who defended the Vatican and proposed national reconciliation after the Occupation, he encouraged Jewish writers to tell their stories of the Holocaust. His writing life, which first blossomed in *fin de siècle* Paris, went on to span both world wars and the end of France's colonial interests. During the Warsaw Uprising, Czapski published an open letter to Mauriac, a friend of twenty years, and Jacques Maritain, both models of humanitarianism and Christian compassion. He pleaded with them to raise their voices against the Nazi slaughter of Polish citizens. Neither man responded.

ADAM MICKIEWICZ (1798–1855)
Polish poet
Occupying a supremely elevated position in the pantheon of Polish poets, Mickiewicz was a romantic who combined great powers of imagination with a tender capacity for human feeling and a love of the natural world. He created a large body of work ranging from epic poems to pastoral sonnets to political tracts. The characters peopling his verse are mythic— a Lithuanian princess who dons a man's uniform to confront the Teutonic powers oppressing her people, a nobleman who seeks redemption posing as a monk, the chief of a powerful order who discovers his humble origins. Their exploits reflect the rise of patriotic nationalism throughout Europe and especially in the hearts and minds of the Polish diaspora. A student of Hegel and a friend of Chopin, Mickiewicz exploited his celebrity to act as a representative voice for the freedom of all nations, while simultaneously symbolizing the struggle for freedom of one nation in particular, Poland.

ROBERT DE MONTESQUIOU (1855–1921)
French poet, critic, and aesthete
A descendant of the one of the models for d'Artagnan in *The Three Musketeers* by Dumas, Comte Robert de Montesquiou-Fézensac is probably best remembered for having been the chief inspiration for Proust's character the Baron de Charlus, and the model for the aesthete Jean des Esseintes in Joris-Karl Huysman's novel *À rebours*. Known for his flowery verse and dandyish behavior and appearance, Montesquiou was extremely well connected in Parisian circles, numbering among his friends Sarah Bernhardt, Maurice Barrès, and Edmond de Goncourt. He was a mercurial character, needy and insecure at times, overbearing and vindictive at others.

PAUL MORAND (1888–1976)
French writer and diplomat
A handsome, Oxford-educated embassy attaché whose stories and novellas were much in demand, Paul Morand developed a large following after the First World War. Proust, finding him attractive, was disposed to admire his writing. *Tendres Stocks*, a collection of Morand's short pieces, was published in 1921 with a preface by Proust, who largely ignored the contents of the book he was introducing. In his "Ode to Proust," Morand mocked the novelist's perpetual claims of being on the verge of death. Proust died a few months after it was published. During the Second World War, Morand abandoned the Free French in London and aligned himself with the Vichy regime. When, in 1968, he was elected to the Académie française, Charles de Gaulle refused to receive him at the presidential palace.

ELIZA ORZESZKOWA (1841–1910)
Polish novelist and social critic

A nineteenth-century proto-feminist writer, Orzeszkowa published thirty novels dealing with the themes of marriage, illegitimate children, working conditions for women, and prostitution. A Polish noblewoman, she also championed the rights of the Jewish population of Poland. Her dominant passions were the education of the Polish populace and the independence of Poland, but she died before the founding of the Second Polish Republic in 1918. As a precondition for independence, she always advocated for a strengthening of Polish culture and institutions in place of the ceaseless, unproductive resistance to Russian domination. Orzeszkowa lived and worked under surveillance by the czarist secret police. She oversaw the running of a bookshop and publishing house until both were closed by the Russian authorities.

CHARLES PÉGUY (1873–1914)
French essayist and poet

Péguy was an intellectually driven socialist who had grown up in poverty, among laboring people he admired enormously. His rural childhood gave him a different frame of reference from most French literary figures. His early spiritual poems, inspired by Bergson and Rolland, found wide readership. Péguy's play about Joan of Arc, written in the style of a medieval drama, reflected the writer's immersion in theological mysteries. His work was informed by an almost mystical identification with France. The favorite writer of Charles de Gaulle, Péguy died in battle in the First World War.

RAYMOND RADIGUET (1903–1923)
French writer
Radiguet was only twenty when he died of typhoid fever. His first novel, *Le Diable au corps* (*The Devil in the Flesh*) was provocative; while her husband is away at the front, a young woman carries on an affair with a sixteen-year-old boy. The subject was certainly controversial among soldiers who had returned home from the war. The story may have been autobiographical, and his bold descriptions of the boy's sensuality caused some sensation. His second novel, *Le Bal du Comte d'Orgel* (*Count Orgel's Ball*), referred to by Czapski, was published posthumously, in 1924, when Radiguet would have been just twenty-one. It, too, was provocative in its treatment of adultery. Radiguet and Jean Cocteau were widely known as a couple in Parisian cultural circles, and were lovers at the time of his death, but he also had taken women as lovers, some of whom supported him financially. Coco Chanel supervised his funeral.

ROMAIN ROLLAND (1866–1944)
French dramatist, historian, and novelist
Rolland had a long and diverse career, writing biographies of Tolstoy, Gandhi, and Robespierre, as well as the internationally popular ten-volume roman-fleuve *Jean-Christophe*. Fascinated by eastern mysticism, he entered into a long correspondence with Freud, which had a considerable effect upon the development of *Civilization and its Discontents*. Hermann Hesse dedicated his novel of spiritual awakening, *Siddhartha*, to Rolland. Described by Stefan Zweig as "the moral consciousness of Europe," Rolland was the recipient of the 1915 Nobel Prize for Literature. As teenagers, Czapski and his sister Maria wrote a letter of gratitude to Rolland

and, unexpectedly, received a reply from him, long cherished by them.

VASILY ROZANOV (1856–1919)
Russian philosopher and writer

A thinker struggling with internal contradictions, Rozanov was a controversial figure during the last decades of Imperial Russia. During the dark times following the Russian revolution, Rozanov died of starvation in a monastery. His writings were personal, religious, and aphoristic. In addition to art and theology, he introduced human sexuality as a subject worthy of celebration at a time when Russian Orthodoxy generally forbade public discussion of such topics. He wrestled with the difference between ancient religions and Christianity, lapsing occasionally into anti-Semitic diatribe, referring to Jews as "a little people" who don't speak "the language of Europe." He also claimed that this same people had been solely responsible for bringing civilization to Europe and remained among its most cultivated citizens. His work was praised by a group of artists in Petrograd known as the "decadents." In the 1930s, Czapski was compiling an anthology of Rozanov's writings but this work did not survive the war; a long essay he was writing at the same time was published in expanded form in 1957. In 1964, a selection from Rozanov's works appeared in French translation as *La Face sombre du Christ* (*The Dark Face of Christ*); Czapski provided a sixty-two-page introductory essay.

LOUIS DE ROUVROY (Duc de Saint-Simon; 1675–1755)
French aristocrat, soldier, diplomat

The multiple volumes of Saint-Simon's *Mémoires* concern life at Versailles during the long reign of Louis XIV. The work is renowned for its literary style, and Saint-Simon's vivid descriptions of life at court and its countless intrigues had a powerful impact on writers such as Flaubert and Tolstoy. Proust was a great admirer of the master's touch, with which Saint-Simon could turn a dull report of banal events into a passage of a dazzling observation. He committed long passages from *Mémoires* to memory. Czapski, himself a copious diarist, was also an enthusiast.

ARY SCHEFFER (1795–1858)
French painter of German-Dutch origin
Scheffer moved from Amsterdam to France as an adolescent; after completing a course of study at the École des Beaux-Arts in Paris, he began exhibiting at the Salon. A commissioned portrait of the Marquis de Lafayette launched his career. Literary subjects, portraits, and religious tableaux form the body of his work. Without embracing the romantic fever sweeping through the literary and visual arts, he painted in a style that falls short of the clarity of classicism. Czapski found Scheffer's figures lifeless.

GENEVIÈVE STRAUS (1849–1926)
French salon hostess
Born Geneviève Halévy, she was one of two daughters of Fromental Halévy, composer of the grand opera *La Juive*. She married her father's pupil, Georges Bizet, composer of the opera *Carmen*. He died of a heart attack at thirty-seven. To keep up her spirits, she began to host a salon that drew a remarkable assortment of artists and society people. Proust, a childhood friend of her son Jacques Bizet, gained access to this elite gathering as a very young man. The renowned wit of the Guermantes is really a transcription of the conversation

the young Proust overheard among the Halévys. After her second marriage, to Émile Straus, her salon, one of the finest of the Belle Époque, gained more prominence, but soon the fierce disagreements engendered by the Dreyfus Affair took a toll on its attendance. Madame Straus was the aunt of Czapski's close friend, historian Daniel Halévy.

JEAN-LOUIS VAUDOYER (1883–1963)
French critic and art historian
Poet, museum curator, novelist, Vaudoyer made his mark in the artistic and intellectual milieu of early twentieth-century Paris. He provided Diaghilev with the idea for the ballet *Le Spectre de la rose*, mounted by the Ballets Russes, thus inspiring a seminal work of modern dance. Proust often accompanied Vaudoyer to the theatre, dance, and opera, and together they went to an exhibition of Dutch paintings that had been sent to Paris as a benefit for the city of Flanders, devastated during the First World War. During this gallery visit, Proust was dazzled by Vermeer's *View of Delft*; his sighting of a "little patch of yellow wall" would have an enormous impact on his novel. A brother-in-law of Daniel Halévy, Vaudoyer would serve as director of several cultural institutions, including the Musée Carnavalet and the Comédie Française. During the Second World War he actively collaborated with the Nazis.

AUGUSTE VILLIERS DE L'ISLE-ADAM (1838–1889)
French writer of stories, plays, and poems
Impoverished descendant of an aristocratic family, Villiers de l'Isle-Adam revered Baudelaire, who introduced him to the poetry of Edgar Allan Poe. Greatly influenced by the American writer's gothic romances, Villiers de l'Isle-Adam

wrote his own tales of horror and mysterious, dramatic stories that only found acclaim after his death. His collections *Contes cruels* (*Cruel Tales*) and *Nouveaux Contes cruels*, published in 1883 and 1888, are considered a genre of their own making. His work was championed by Mallarmé and Joris-Karl Huysmans; Villiers de l'Isle-Adam died a pauper.

STEFAN ŻEROMSKI (1864–1925)
Polish novelist and playwright
An internationally renowned writer in his time, Żeromski disappeared from view soon after the emergence of the Second Polish Republic in 1918, when modernism and symbolism began to eclipse the more romantic sensibility of nineteenth-century Polish literature. In the landscape of a timeless Poland, Żeromski's characters are champions of reform, figures who had hardly found a place in earlier fiction. A Byronic figure, prestigious and influential, Żeromski chose to write about the outsider, earning him the distinction of being called "the conscience" of Polish literature. Czapski, an admirer, met Żeromski near the end of the writer's life and always held him in high esteem.

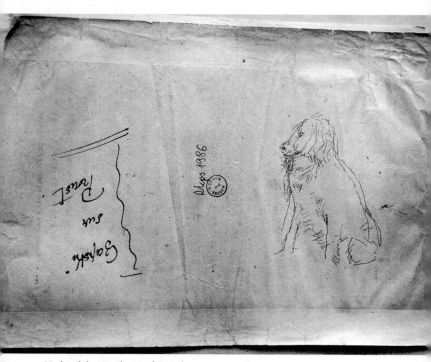

Undated drawing by Józef Czapski.

ACKNOWLEDGMENTS

I WOULD like to express my appreciation to Vera Michalski and Éditions Noir sur Blanc for the use of photographic plates of Czapski's diagrams, the originals of which have not been seen since 1987. Éditions Noir sur Blanc is also the publisher of Sabine Mainberger and Neil Stewart's compelling study of Czapski's Gryazovets notebooks, *À la recherche de* La Recherche.

Janusz Nowak sanctioned my research at the Princes Czartoryski Library in Kraków and inspired me in his devotion to Czapski's journals. Guillaume Perrier and Agnieszka Żuk's article "Mémoire involontaire et détail mnémotechnique: Czapski lecteur de Proust" appeared in *Écrire l'histoire*, no. 3, 2009. Many of my ideas found a sympathetic resonance there. James Connelly graciously shared with me his own treatment of Czapski's lectures.

Almost fifty years ago, I was first welcomed into the world of *À la recherche* as a seventeen-year-old student of Dr. Stephan Ethe. He could not have predicted the place Proust would come to occupy in my life, but he would have understood.

More than a generation younger than I, Mikołaj Nowak-Rogoziński is an example of the ongoing power of Czapski's appeal and its ability to speak across time and space. His help has been illuminating and invaluable, managing to restore my confidence in the term gentleman-scholar. I'm very much indebted to him.

Steven Barclay put a volume of Czapski's lectures on Proust into my hands. The gift was unexpected and life-transforming. What more can one ask of a friend?

Performing various roles, Wojciech Karpiński and Michael Sell ably assisted in the production of this book.

OTHER NEW YORK REVIEW CLASSICS

For a complete list of titles, visit www.nyrb.com or write to:
Catalog Requests, NYRB, 435 Hudson Street, New York, NY 10014

RENATA ADLER Speedboat*
ROBERT AICKMAN Compulsory Games*
CÉLESTE ALBARET Monsieur Proust
JEAN AMÉRY Charles Bovary, Country Doctor*
KINGSLEY AMIS Lucky Jim*
EVE BABITZ Slow Days, Fast Company: The World, the Flesh, and L.A.*
HONORÉ DE BALZAC The Human Comedy: Selected Stories*
MIRON BIAŁOSZEWSKI A Memoir of the Warsaw Uprising*
ADOLFO BIOY CASARES The Invention of Morel
PAUL BLACKBURN (TRANSLATOR) Proensa*
LESLEY BLANCH Journey into the Mind's Eye: Fragments of an Autobiography*
ROBERT BRESSON Notes on the Cinematograph*
JOHN HORNE BURNS The Gallery
ROBERT BURTON The Anatomy of Melancholy
MATEI CALINESCU The Life and Opinions of Zacharias Lichter*
DON CARPENTER Hard Rain Falling*
LEONORA CARRINGTON Down Below*
EILEEN CHANG Little Reunions*
JÓZEF CZAPSKI Inhuman Land: A Wartime Journey through the USSR*
TIBOR DÉRY Niki: The Story of a Dog
ALFRED DÖBLIN Berlin Alexanderplatz*
MAVIS GALLANT Paris Stories*
NATALIA GINZBURG Family Lexicon*
NIKOLAI GOGOL Dead Souls*
EDMOND AND JULES DE GONCOURT Pages from the Goncourt Journals
ALICE GOODMAN History Is Our Mother: Three Libretti*
JULIEN GRACQ Balcony in the Forest*
HENRY GREEN Loving*
VASILY GROSSMAN Life and Fate*
ELIZABETH HARDWICK The Collected Essays of Elizabeth Hardwick*
PAUL HAZARD The Crisis of the European Mind: 1680–1715*
ALICE HERDAN-ZUCKMAYER The Farm in the Green Mountains*
WOLFGANG HERRNDORF Sand*
BOHUMIL HRABAL Dancing Lessons for the Advanced in Age*
DOROTHY B. HUGHES In a Lonely Place*
YASUSHI INOUE Tun-huang*
TOVE JANSSON The Summer Book*
UWE JOHNSON Anniversaries*
WALTER KEMPOWSKI All for Nothing
TOM KRISTENSEN Havoc*
GIUSEPPE TOMASI DI LAMPEDUSA The Professor and the Siren
PATRICK LEIGH FERMOR A Time of Gifts*
SIMON LEYS The Hall of Uselessness: Collected Essays*
CURZIO MALAPARTE The Kremlin Ball
JANET MALCOLM In the Freud Archives
JEAN-PATRICK MANCHETTE Ivory Pearl*
OSIP MANDELSTAM The Selected Poems of Osip Mandelstam

* *Also available as an electronic book.*